Kanthapura to Malgudi

Cultural Values and Assumptions in Selected South Indian Novelists in English

In the same series

Indian Literature Today ((2 vols.)
R.K. Dhawan, ed.

Recent Indian Fiction
R.S. Pathak, ed.

New Perspectives on Indian Writing
V.L.V.N. Narendra Kumar

Comparative Perspectives on Indian Literature
A. Ramakrishna Rao, ed.

Man-Woman Relationship in Indian Fiction
Seema Suneel

Major Indian Novelists
K. Venkata Reddy

Five Indian Novelists
B. Rajan, Raja Rao, R.K. Narayan, Anita Desai and Arun joshi
V.V.N. Rajendra Prasad

Style in Indian English Fiction
Z.N. Patil

Kanthapura to Malgudi

Cultural Values and Assumptions in Selected South Indian Novelists in English

S. Xavier Alphonse, S.J.

Sangam Books

SANGAM BOOKS LIMITED
57 London Fruit Exchange
Brushfield Street
London E1 6EP, U.K.

By arrangement with
PRESTIGE BOOKS
3/28, East Patel Nagar
New Delhi 110 008

ISBN: 0 86132 386 6

Composed by Pivot Computers, Delhi 110 006
Printed by Mehra Offset Press, New Delhi 110 002

Dedicated to
my beloved parents
Late Mrs. E. MARY RAJAM
MR. SWAMIKANNU
and
to the beloved MOTHER
THE SOCIETY OF JESUS
in particular the
MADURAI JESUIT PROVINCE
for all that they have given to me
to make the person that I am to-day

Contents

Part III

The Cultural Approach: The South Indian Element

Part IV

The Cultural Values and Assumptions

The Idea and Role of Womanhood

The Significance of Relationship

The Role of Myths and Puranas

The Absorption of Native Proverbs, Expressions, Festivals and Customs

The Role of the Guru and Asceticism

The Role of Bhakti and the Idea of Religion

Part V

The List of Charts

Preface

The present book deals with the cultural study of the selected South Indian Novelists in English from 1925 to 1985. It is an extensive as well as an in-depth study of the cultural values and assumptions found in their novels. My sincere concern is to explore whether these novelists truly and authentically represent the South Indian culture and ethos to both the native as well as foreign readers. The novels of these fiction writers are used as a means of communication with Indians as well as western readers to give them an account of the South Indian culture. The novels also become vehicles of self-expression in which the English language itself gets integrated and adapted into the text of the novels.

Many individuals and institutions have helped me in the production of this book. I am grateful to:

Dr. Francis Soundararajan, Former Principal of Madras Christian College, Madras who was my research guide;

Dr. Spellman, Chairman, Asian Institute of Cultures, University of Windsor, Canada for his personal interest and insistence on accuracy and sharpness of the ideas;

The provincials of Madurai Jesuit Province, Fr. Michael Jeyaraj, S.J and Fr. Aloysius Irudayam;

The Principals of St. Joseph's College (Autonomous) Tiruchirapalli, Fr. Gnanarethinam, Fr. M. Sebastian, Fr. Mathew Moolel;

The Jesuit community at St. Joseph's College, Tiruchy and Loyola College, Madras;

The Jesuits of George Town University, Washington, Boston College, Loyola University of Chicago, Detroit Province in U.S.A;

The librarians of the University of Chicago, Sahitya Akademi, New Delhi, Central Institute of English, Hyderabad;

The British Council, Madras, especially and Mr. Bellarmine, Special Officer who gave me a visitorship grant for six months in U.K during 1987-88;

Dr. Prema Nandakumar, Dr. Meenakshi Mukherjee, Prof. C.D.Narasimhaiah for their thought-provoking and challenging interviews;

The noted novelist David Lodge, Dr. Alistair Niven, the Director of Arts and Literature in Great Britain, Prof. William Walsh, Prof. Arthur Ravenscroft, Prof. Marilyn Butler, Dr. Shirley Chew, Dr. David Richards for their meaningful and insightful discussion on my doctoral thesis during my visit to Great Britain and the Universities of London, Oxford, Cambridge, Leeds, Birmingham and York;

Dr. Kolangaden and Dr. Sundararaman, the Heads of Departments of English of St. Joseph's College, Tiruchy and Dr. V.J. Mathew, the Head of the Department of English, Loyola College, Madras;

Dear colleagues of the departments of English of St. Joseph's and Loyola;

Mr. James Melchior, my loving brother for all his insights and contributions;

Mrs. Bala Salomon, my youngerst sister, and Mr. Salomon, my brother-in-law, and Miss Vandana for helping me to edit my work;

My good friend Dr. R.K. Dhawan who inspired me to get this book published;

Mr. Xavier Britto, a dear brother of mine who helped me in the publication of this book;

Ms. D. Renu and all her colleagues at the Prestige Books for bringing out the book so elegantly and expeditiously.

All the readers and scholars who, I believe, will find the present book interesting and useful.

Introduction

Indian English literature has been accepted as an integral part of Indian, Commonwealth and English literatures. Indian English fiction forms the bulk of Indian English literature. More than three hundred novels have been written in English by Indian novelists from 1864 till the present day. The critics in India as well as abroad have been very enterprising and creative in suggesting different critical approaches to Indian English fiction. The present work is an attempt to focus the cultural approach, i.e. to add a new thrust to this critical approach by making it more specific and particular in the study of selected South Indian novelists in English. Without understanding and evaluating the strong regional and cultural element in these authors, there is every likelihood, we miss the richness, variety, depth and specificity of the novels.

The Aim and Scope of the Book

The aim of the book is to elaborate the focusing of the cultural approach to Indian English fiction, to interpret and evaluate the South Indian cultural element in the selected South Indian novelists in English. The book will focus on analysing not merely the cultural values and assumptions from the distinctive point of view of being South Indian but also will explore the different ways and emphasis with which these novelists present them. The selected South Indian novelists and their novels chosen for analysis are given in the chart on page 15.

In the novelists chosen for our study, the novels are used as a means of communication with Indians as well as western readers to give them an account of the South Indian culture and certain changes that are taking place within the traditional cultural values and assumptions. The novels also become vehicles of self expression in which the English language itself gets integrated and adapted into the text of the novels. These issues will be dealt within the book.

The Five Parts of the Book

The first part deals with Indian English literature in general with some of its problems. It touches briefly on the following problems: (a) the gradual acceptance and recognition of Indian English literature as a part of Indian, Commonwealth and English literatures, amidst controversies (b) the various names used to designate this branch of literature Anglo-Indian, Indo-Anglian, Indo-English (c) 'Indianness' being the distinctive quality of this literature and the difficulty in defining this concept (d) the problems of language and subject matter faced by the Indian creative writers in English and their testimonies regarding the reconciliation of these problems in their own writing. This introductory part provides a meaningful backdrop for the discussion of the Indian English fiction and the South Indian novelists in English.

The second part describes and comments on the critical approaches taken in India as well as abroad to study the Indian English fiction: (a) the historical-biographical (b) the thematic (c) the Indian 'aesthetic' (d) the formalistic which includes the linguistic aspect of the novels (e) the sociological and cultural approach where the novels serve as documents of cultural knowledge.

The third part introduces the aim of the present study which is an extension as well as the focusing of the cultural approach, restricting it to the selected South Indian novelists in English. The cultural approach is used with a new thrust to identify the peculiar and the distinctive South Indian cultural values and assumptions. The meaning and the definition of the terms of the thesis: Culture, Values, Assumptions, South Indian novelists in English and the reasons for the selection of these novelists, are explained.

The fourth part focuses on the specific South Indian cultural element. The cultural values and assumptions depicted by the selected novelists are wide-ranging. The following are chosen for our discussion and analysis, representing a few vital aspects of the culture in South India.

a) Social Expression: the idea and role of womanhood and the significance of relationship.
b) Literary and Traditional Aspects: the role of myths and puranas and the absorption of Tamil expressions, proverbs and customs into the narrative.
c) The religious and cultural manifestations: the role of the Guru and Asceticism and the role of Bhakti and the idea of religion.

The concluding part will enunciate a few critical observations in judging and evaluating the South Indian novelists in English based on the analysis of each of the above cultural values and assumptions.

The Selected South Indian Novelists and the Novels Chosen for Analysis with the Years of Publication*

1.	K.S. Venkataramani	*Murugan, the Tiller* (1927); *Kandan, the Patriot* (1932)
2.	K. Nagarajan	*Athawar House* (1939); *The Chronicles of Kedaram* (1961)
3.	R.K. Narayan	*Swami and His Friends* (1935); *The Bachelor of Arts* (1937); *The Dark Room* (1938); *The English Teacher* (1945); *Mr. Sampath, the Printer of Malgudi* (1949); *The Financial Expert* (1952); *Waiting for the Mahatma* (1955); *The Guide* (1958); *The Man-Eater of Malgudi* (1961); *The Vendor of Sweets* (1976); *The Painter of Signs* (1976); *A Tiger for Malgudi* (1983); *Talkative Man* (1986)
4.	Raja Rao	*Kanthapura* (1938); *The Serpent and the Rope* (1960); *The Cat and Shakespeare: A Tale of India* (1965) *Comrade Kirillov* (1976) *The Chessmaster and His Moves* (1988)
5.	Kamala Markandaya	*Nectar in a Sieve* (1954); *Some Inner Fury* (1955); *A Silence of Desire* (1960); *Possession* (1963); *A Handful of Rice* (1966); *The Coffer Dams* (1969); *The Nowhere Man* (1972); *Two Virgins* (1973); *The Golden Honeycomb* (1977); *Pleasure City* (1982)
6.	Santha Rama Rau	*Remember the House* (1956); *The Adventuress* (1970)
7.	Balachandra Rajan	*The Dark Dancer* (1959); *Too Long in the West* (1961)

* Seven Authors and Thirty Six Novels

Part I

Indian English Literature: Some Problems

Indian English literature has gained gradual acceptance and recognition both in India as well as abroad, over the last fifty years. This gradual acceptance had not been without its share of problems and controversies: the debate that goes on even to-day about its viability and validity at the national and international level especially in Writers Conferences; the various names by which Indian English literature has been known; the difficulty of defining the concept of "Indianness"; the problems of language and subject-matter faced by the creative Indian writers in English.

1.1 The Problem of Gradual Acceptance

Indian English literature has been accepted as a part of Indian literature and English literature. This is evident in the testimonies of the writers and academics, published by the national and international writers' conferences.

At the writers' conference in Jaipur, 1945, Nirmal Kumar Sidhanta defends the case of Indian English literature and the tone is one of accusation and defence: "In speaking of English literature produced by Indians during this generation, I feel handicapped as the speakers on the other literatures have not been! I feel that I have to be on my defence, as there are charges constantly brought forward against creative artists who have chosen English as the medium of expression."[1]

The important charge against the Indian writers in English is that the English language is not a natural medium of expression for the Indian writer.[2] One could feel the hesitation and diffidence on the part of N.K. Sidhanta in pleading for the acceptance of Indian English literature.

Indian writing in English gains considerable international acceptance and recognition when K.R. Srinivasa Iyengar is invited to the University of Leeds to give a series of lectures on 'Indian Writing in English' in January, 1959. In his inaugural lecture of this series, he expresses his surprise and joy at the recognition awarded to Indian English literature: "Your decision to start in your University a course in the various literatures produced in English in the commonwealth countries and to inaugurate this commendable project with the present series of lectures on Indian writing in English came to me as to many of my friends in India as a pleasant surprise."[3]

He also stated in the same lecture that Indian English literature is a part of Indian literature. Indian literature comprises several literatures. . . . Indian writing in English is but one of the voices in which India speaks. It is a new voice, no doubt but it is as much Indian as the others."[4] K.R. Srinivasa Iyengar has the credit of working for the recognition of Indian English literature at the national and international levels. His plea that Indian writing in English is a part of Indian literature reveals the fact that the creative Indian writers in English were not accepted by their contemporaries, the writers of the regional languages of India.

C.D. Narasimhaiah refers to the status given to Indian English literature as a part of commonwealth literature (First Commonwealth Conference of Writers, University of Leeds, 9-12 September, 1964).[5] He insisted on the process of cross-fertilization that takes place in the Indian writer in English who participates in Indian as well as Western traditions: "An Indian who writes in English is also the heir to the two traditions, Indian and Western."[6]

The national acceptance and recognition to Indian English literature in India is noticeable in the Seminar on "Indian Writing in English" held at the University of Mysore, January 13-16, 1968. This change in the attitude of the Indian scholars and critics towards Indian English literature is perceived by A. Wendt, a participant from England: "To an observer from the Western world, the Seminar on Indian writing in English held at Mysore University in January of 1968, marked an important milestone along the road to general acceptance and appreciation of an important branch of world literature. Regrettably but perhaps understandably, Indian scholars and critics have been slow to evaluate this branch of literature."[7]

The Conference was not without controversy. Subba Rao raised his dissenting voice expressing his belief that the choice of English for creative writing had social and self-seeking implications. According to him, English has always been the language of the urban rich and the educated classes, who represent a kind of life that is "un-Indian." He asserted that he values only Indian literature as an expression of Indian culture and here the Indian writing in English has failed.[8] He contended that it is one's own language that can be the natural and appropriate medium for literary expression. Since English is not our language, our writers cannot express their deepest and inmost thoughts in it. A sense of vanity and a desire to be fashionable are the motives which govern the creation of Indian writing in English. Hence, all Indian fiction writers in English are "a very inferior breed of authors."[9] Thus he questioned the viability and validity of the Indian writing in English. Some of these questions are debated even to-day. Balarama Gupta, the editor of *Journal of Indian Writing in English,* attempted to answer the charges of Subba Rao against Indian writers in English.[10]

The contribution of the Indian writers in English to the development of the English language in India is acknowledged by Alistair Niven, the editor of the *Journal of Commonwealth Literature* in these words: "We have left our language here (India). You have done new things with it, producing writers who use it with freshness and confidence."[11]

The gradual acceptance and recognition of Indian English literature as a part of Indian literature and English literatures both at the national and at the international levels, has come slowly amidst controversies to the present day.

1.2 The Problem of the Name

Indian writing in English has been designated by different names: Anglo-Indian, Indo-Anglian, Indo-English and Indian English.

(i) Anglo-Indian: In 1908, E.F. Oaten won a prize at Cambridge for his essay on Anglo-Indian literature. Later he published it as a book *A Sketch of Anglo-Indian Literature.*[13] In this book, he confined himself to the writings of Englishmen in India, on Indian themes. Primarily, Anglo-Indian literature has been literature produced by Englishmen born in India or while on active service in India or during their trips to India but essentially recounting their Indian experience. This would include authors such as E.M. Forster, Rudyard Kipling, F.W. Bain, Sir Edwin Arnold, F.A. Steel, John Masters, Paul Scott and others who have written about India.[14] The term has also been used to include Indian writers in English by authors such as Bhupal Singh[15] and George Sampson.[16] This term cannot be used today to describe Indian writing in English because it refers to a particular community in India today.[17]

(ii) Indo-Anglian: This term was coined by J.H. Cousins in 1883.[18] It received general currency and usage by Srinivasa Iyengar.[19] The advantage, according to him, in using this term, is that it can be used both as adjective and substantive. It is reasonably handy and descriptive to describe Indian creative writing in English.[20]

Meenakshi Mukherjee restricts the use of the term Indo-Anglian to include only the writings of those who are Indian and have written in English. She excludes all the works translated into English even when the translation is done by the author himself.[21]

The major flaw in the term 'Indo-Anglian' is pointed out by John Alphonso-Karkala. He maintains that this term suggests more than the relation between two countries, India and England, rather than a country and a language.[22]

An enterprising London printer was puzzled by this odd expression 'Indo-Anglian' and changed it into 'Indo-Anglican.'[23]

(iii) Indo-English: This term was popularized by John Alphonso-Karkala. "Indo-English literature is a unique phenomenon especially considering its origin under accidents of history and its development through the process of emerging nationalism."[24] In the usage of the term, he refers to both the elements that constitute the Indian writing in English: The subject-matter concerning India and the English language used as a medium of expression.

Srinvasa Iyengar finds this term suitable but it cannot be used conveniently both as an adjective as well as substantive.[25] This term has also been used to indicate and describe translations from Indian languages into English by V.K. Gokak.[26] Translations from the Indian languages and literature into English cannot form part of the Indian English literature because the technical, linguistic, artistic problems of a translated work are totally different from those of a work, conceived and created in English.[27]

(iv) Indian English: The Sahitya Akademi, New Delhi, has accepted Indian English as the most suitable and appropriate term to describe the Indian writers in English by its official publication of the book by M.K. Naik, *A History of Indian English Literature* in 1982. The term emphasizes two significant ideas: Indian English literature constitutes one of the many streams of Indian literature and it is an inevitable product of the nativization of the English language to express the Indian sensibility.[28]

Whatever might be the term that is used to describe the Indian writing in English, it has come to be recognized as a part of Indian literature. It has a distinctive and distinguishable quality: the expression of Indian culture, ethos, concerns and pre-occupations broadly classified as 'Indianness.' The defining of the concept of Indianness takes us to the next problem connected with Indian English literature.

1.3 The Problem of Definition: The Concept of Indianness

The concept of 'Indianness' is interpreted differently by different authors: "the sum total of the cultural patterns of India" (Paul Verghese);[29] "the writers' intense awareness of his entire culture" (V.K.Gokak);[30] "the stock images of Indian culture" (Vasant Shahane);[31] "Indianness . . . not a life-style nor a mere vision. It is an instrument, people fashion out . . . in order to maintain a rhythmic balance of their individualistic and cultural existence" (Thakazhi Sivasankaran Pillai);[32] "a perception of the mind" (Samares Sanyal);[33] "a sensibility" (William Walsh).[34]

These divergent attempts to define the concept of Indianness reveal the difficulty in having an accurate and exact definition of the concept. To a large extent, the concept tends to be vague, general and nebulous. A detailed discussion on the difficulty in defining and in marking it as a criterion for judging the Indian English fiction will be dealt with, in the next part. Whatever might be the interpretation of the concept of "Indianness," authors and critics agree broadly on this single factor: The peculiar and distinctive quality of Indian writing in English is the immersion and participation of the Indian writer in English into the culture, ethos and concerns of India.

1.4 The Problems of Subject-Matter and Language

The Indian writer in English faces a few problems in his creative endeavour because of the subject-matter involved and the language he chooses to write.

The obvious problem, the Indian writer in English faces is the presentation of nuances and shades of Indian life through a language that is not of Indian origin. The problem is the suitability and adaptability of English as a medium of expression for the Indian writer in English. This problem is raised by Jyoti Datta, Bengali writer and critic: "How can a writer use a language creatively when all around him another language is being spoken and when the creative centres of the language are thousands of miles away? From where can he receive the feel of the living, changing language.[35]

The gap between the writer and the society and the people about whom he writes, created by the use of the English language is pointed out by Paul Verghese: "The attempt of the Indian novelist in English to depict the life of those whose emotional and intellectual life is fashioned by a different language is characterized by a total absence of the mutual nourishment between the writer and his society."[36]

The next problem the Indian writer in English faces is the choice of the subject-matter. The writer encounters a heterogeneous audience both in India as well as abroad. The English language cuts across diverse ethnic, religious and cultural background. This gives the writer a wider audience but makes him uncertain of his basic themes and assumptions. The recognizable themes applicable to the whole of India are not many in number.[37] Besides there is a great deal of regional variation in social structure, values, customs and problems in different parts of India. This problem will be discussed in detail in the following parts.

The Indian writer in English is also in a predicament to cater to a western audience. Hence the constant accusation against these writers is "Since he writes for a western audience he will inevitably fail to present a true image of India and in as much as in his own interest, he will try to create an image that is most saleable."[38]

1.5 The Testimonies of the Writers

The problem of the language and the subject-matter chosen are dealt with by the writers themselves. Their testimonies attempt to reconcile the thorny problems of the subject-matter about India and the expression of it in a foreign language like English.

Raja Rao, in his famous foreword to *Kanthapura* justifies the presence of these problems in his own creative writing:

> One has to convey in a language that is not one's own, the spirit that is one's own. One has to convey the various shades and omissions of a certain thought movement that looks maltreated in an alien language. I use the word 'alien' yet English is not an alien language to us. It is the language of our intellectual make-up like Sanskrit or Persian was before—but not of our emotional make-up. We are all instinctively bi-lingual, many of us writing in our own language and in English. We cannot write like the English. We should not. We cannot write only as Indians. We have grown to look at the large world as part of us. Our method of expression therefore has to be a dialect which will someday prove to be as distinctive and colourful as the Irish or the American. Time also will justify it . . . the tempo of the Indian life must be infused into our English expression.[39]

R.K. Narayan, one of the veterans in the field of Indian English writing admits that English has enough flexibility, resilience and mobility to yield itself to the process of Indianization and it has served his purpose admirably well: "All that I am able to confirm nearly after thirty years of writing is that it has served my purpose admirably, of conveying unambiguously the thoughts and actions of a set of personalities, who flourish in a small town located in a corner of South India."[40]

"English has been with us for over a century and a half. I am particularly fond of the language. I was never aware that I was using a different foreign language when I wrote in English because it came to me very easily. . . . English is a very adaptable language. And it is so transparent, it can take on the tint of any country."[41]

Mulk Raj Anand, who started writing in English when he was twelve and continues to write, affirms the interactions of the Indian subject-matter and the English language. According to him Indian writing in English is: "A highly dignified literature . . . not to be dismissed as 'Babu' writing in the King-Emperor's English with which it has very little in common because of the mastery it displays over the English language . . . the Indo-Anglian writers may be valued as interpreters and pioneers who brought the techniques of European literature into our country whilst contributing Indian idiom and metaphor to English literature."[42]

The contemporary writers like Bhabani Bhattacharya, Kamala Das and Anita Desai make a passionate plea for the freedom of the creative artist to express oneself through whatever language he or she chooses. "The concept of freedom will have to include the medium of expression to which the writer, out of his inner urge, commits himself. . . . It is far more difficult to write creatively in foreign language than in one's own. But that must be regarded as the writer's own business."[43]

In defence of her choice of English, as the medium of her poetic expression, Kamala Das speaks out with a touch of defiance: "I am an Indian, very brown, born in Malabar. I speak three languages, write in two, dream in one. Don't write English. They said English is not your mother-tongue. Why not leave Me alone, critics, friends, visiting cousins, Everyone of you? Why not let me speak in Any language I like? The language I speak becomes mine, mine alone. It is half-English, half-Indian, funny perhaps but it is honest, it is as human as I am human."[44]

Anita Desai expresses her deliberate choice of English as the medium of her expression: "I am very glad to be writing in a language as rich, as flexible, supple, adaptable, varied and vital as English. . . . It answers my every need. I do believe it is even capable of taking on an Indian flavour, an Indian character, purely by reflection."[45]

Nissim Ezekiel, the noted Indian English poet insists more than the subject-matter and the language, the literary and cultural context. "We can't merely ask how good Narayan or Raja Rao is. We have to describe the literary and cultural context of their work."[46]

These are some of the testimonies of the Indian writers in English to show how they reconcile the subject-matter about India and the English language, they choose as their medium to convey the subject-matter.

This introductory first part touches briefly on some important problems connected with Indian English literature: its gradual acceptance and recognition as a part of Indian Commonwealth and English literature; the various names used to designate this branch of literature: Anglo-Indian, Indo-Anglian, Indo-English, Indian-English; the distinctive quality of this literature being "Indianness" and the difficulty in defining this concept; the problem of language and subject-matter faced by Indian creative writers in English and their testimonies regarding the reconciliation of these problems in their own writing. The aim of this part has been to provide a meaningful backdrop for our further discussion on the critical approaches to Indian English fiction and the cultural values and assumptions in selected South Indian novelists in English.

NOTES

1. N.K. Sidhanta, "English," in *Indian Literature of To-Day:* A Symposium. (The All India Writer's Conference, Jaipur, 1945), ed. Bharata Kumarappa (Calcutta: P.E.N. All India Centre), p. 24.
2. *Ibid.*, p. 24
3. K.R. Srinivasa Iyengar, *Indian Writing in English* (New Delhi: Sterling, 1983), p. 1
4. *Ibid.*, p. 3.
5. C.D. Narasimhaiah, "Commonwealth Literature and National Identity," *Two Cheers for Commonwealth*, ed. K.R. Srinivasa Iyengar (Bombay: Asia, 1970), p. 44.
6. C.D. Narasimhaiah, "Commonwealth Literature: Soundings and Markings," *Two Cheers for Commonwealth*, p. 16.
7. A. Wendt, "Summary Account of the Seminar on Indian Writing in English, Mysore University 13-16,1968," *Indian Literature of the Past Fifty Years,* ed. C.D. Narasimhaiah (Mysore: University of Mysore, 1970), p. 344.
8. *Ibid.*, p. 346.
9. T.V. Subba Rao, *Indian Writing in English: Is There Any Worth In It* (Madurai: Koodal, 1976), p. 20.
10. Balarama Gupta, "Indian Writing in English: Is There Any Worth in It?" *Journal of South Asian Literature* (Formerly MAHFIL), 16:2. (Summer & Fall 1981), p. 176

11. Sahitya Akademi, "Seminar on Indian Literature in English and English Translation," *Indian Literature*, 29,113 (May-June 1986), pp. 135-36.
12. Srinivasa Iyengar, *Indian Writing in English*, p. 2.
13. Edward Farley Oaten, *A Sketch of Anglo-Indian Literature* (London: Kegan Paul, Trench, Trubner, 1908).
14. John B. Alphonse-Karkala and Leena Karkala, *Bibliography of Indo-English Literature* (Bombay: Nirmal Sadanand, 1974), Introduction, p. 5.
15. M.K. Naik, *A History of Indian English Literature* (New Delhi: Sahitya Akademi, 1982), p. 2.
16. Vasant Shahane, "Indo-English Literature: Its Major Concerns and Its Academic Rationale," *Alien Voice: Perspectives on Commonwealth Literature*, Avadhesh K. Srivastava (Lucknow: Print House, 1981), p. 9.
17. Meenakshi Mukherjee, *The Twice-Born Fiction* (New Delhi: Arnold Heinemann, 1971), p. 14.
18. M.K. Naik, *A History of Indian English Literature*, p. 4.
19. *Ibid.*
20. K.R. Srinivasa Iyengar, *Indian Writing in English*, p. 4.
21. Meenakshi Mukerjee, *The Twice-Born Fiction*, p. 14.
22. M.K. Naik, *A History of Indian English Literature*, p. 4.
23. K.R. Srinivasa Iyengar, *Indian Writing in English*, pp. 3-4.
24. John B. Alphonse-Karkala and Leena Karkala, *Bibliography of Indo-English literature*, pp. 5-6.
25. Srinivasa Iyengar, *Indian Writing in English*, p. 4.
26. M.K. Naik, *A History of Indian English Literature*, p. 2.
27. *Ibid.*, pp. 2-3.
28. *Ibid.*, p. 5.
29. Paul Verghese, *Essays on Indian Writing in English* (New Delhi: N.V. Publishers, 1975), p. 3.
30. V.K. Gokak, "The Concept of Indianness with reference to Indian Writing in English," *Indian Writing in English*, ed. Ramesh Mohan (New Delhi: Orient Longman, 1978), p. 24.
31. Vasant A. Shahane, "Indo-English Literature," p. 13.
32. Thakazhi Sivasankaran Pillai, "Indianness in Literature," *Indian Literature*, 29, 111 (1986), p. 66 (Translated from Malayalam by K. Narayana Chandran).
33. Samares C. Sanyal, *Indianness in Major Indo-Anglian Novels* (Bareilly: Prakash, 1984), p. 265.
34. William Walsh, "The Indian Sensibility in English," *Awakened Conscience: Studies in Commonwealth Literature*, ed. C.D. Narasimhaiah (New Delhi: Sterling, 1978), p. 71.
35. David McCutchion, *Indian Writing in English: Critical Essays* (Calcutta: Writers Workshop, 1969), p. 26.
36. Paul Verghese, *Problems of the Indian Creative Writer in English* (Bombay: Somaiya, 1971), p. 98.
37. Meenakshi Mukherjee, *The Twice-Born Fiction*, p. 99.

38. Paul Verghese, *Problems of the Indian Creative Writer in English*, p. 98.
39. Raja Rao, *Kanthapura* (London: Oxford University Press, 1963).
40. John Press, ed., *Commonwealth Literature: Unity and Diversity in a Common Culture* (London: Heinemann Educational Books, 1965).
41. P.S. Sundaram, *R.K. Narayan* (New Delhi: Arnold-Heinemann, 1973), p. 131.
42. Mulk Raj Anand, *The King Emperor's English or the Role of the English Language in the Free India* (Bombay: Hind Kitab, 1948), pp. 18-19.
43. Iqbal Bakhtiyar, ed., *The Novel in Modern India* (Bombay: The P.E.N. All India Centre, 1964), p. 43.
44. Kamala Das "Introduction," in *The Golden Treasury of Indo-Anglian Poetry*, ed. V.K. Gokak (New Delhi, 1970), p. 240.
45. *Ibid.*
46. N.D. Dani, "An Interview with Nizzim Ezekiel," *Journal of Indian Writing in English*, 14:2 (June-July 1986), p. 118.

Part II

Indian English Fiction
Critical Approaches: A Review

2.1 Indian English Fiction: The Bulk of Indian English Literature

Indian English fiction forms the bulk of Indian English literature from the later part of the nineteenth century to the present day. The comprehensive bibliography of Indian English literature in the nineteenth century of Alphonso Karkala refers to 33 collections of poetry in contrast to the 25 works of fiction: sketches, legends, short stories and novels.[1] In the first three decades of the twentieth century, relatively a few Indian English novels were published (about 26 titles) compared to a great number of books that came into market afterwards (up to 1970, 180 titles).[2] In the seventies and eighties, there are novelists who are writing even to-day such as Anita Desai, Nayantara Sahgal, Manohar Malgonkar, Arun Joshi, Ruskin Bond, Bharati Mukherjee, Chaman Nahal, Raji Narasimhan, Romen Basu, Veena Paintal, Nergis Dalal and M.V. Rama Sarma.[3]

2.2 The Novel, a Western Literary Form Comes to India

The novel as a western form comes into India in the later part of the nineteenth century. "The novel as a medium of story-telling and art-form is essentially of the west and represents a tradition of fictional writing which is totally different from India's time-honoured tradition of story-telling which is essentially an oral one."[4] The first Indian English novel *Rajmohan's Wife* (1864) by Bankim Chandra was published in West Bengal.[5] "Bankim was a true pioneer of the Indian novel in English in the sense that he produced a novel which demonstrated that it was possible to write about Indian life and to describe Indian scenes in a foreign language without becoming imitative."[6] He was able to adapt alien form and medium to a theme and sensibility which were essentially Indian. The novel *Rajmohan's Wife* is the story of an ill-treated wife who seeks her release from the cruelties and tyrannies of a medieval past.[7]

2.3 The Genesis of the Indian English Novel

The beginning of Indian English literature especially Indian English fiction depended on the propagation of the English language in India. This underwent a faster development in the first part of the nineteenth century for these reasons[8]:

a) The European enlightenment found an enthusiastic echo among Indian intellectuals especially in Bengal. Looking at the Western example, they demanded social and religious reforms and wrote mostly in English to reach the English public and government. The leader of this movement was Raja Rammohan Roy (1772-1833) who in his essays, pamphlets and petitions spoke out against Sati, child marriage, religious fanaticism and dogmatism and against the social discrimination and exploitation of women. Indian historians like to call this movement the "Indian Renaissance" or "The Indian Enlightenment."

"English was used rather for utilitarian than for aesthetic purposes. Indo-English fiction did not exist at this time" (Klaus Steinworth)

b) The Christian missions quickly spread and used English for instruction in church and school. For a long time, they were the only institutions furthering the development of English as the East India Company was not specially interested in matters of culture and education.
c) In 1835, Macaulay's "Minute on Education" initiated the government's conscious effort in propagating more rapidly the use of English for educational purposes.[9]

With the gradual progress of school education in English, experimental compositions of Indian creative writing in English, soon appeared. They were mostly exercises in a foreign language.[10] Interest was evinced at the Hindu College in Calcutta in the study of the admired masters of English poetry such as Shakespeare, Wordsworth, Byron, Scott and Tennyson. A number of poems were published which were largely imitations of these great masters of English literature.[11]

Works of fiction appeared only later, in the second part of the nineteenth century. They were merely sketches, narratives, legends, more or less disguised autobiographies which presented scenes of Indian life to rouse the interest of the English public.[12]

The rise of the novel in its developed form in the later half of the nineteenth century was not purely a literary phenomenon. It was a social phenomenon that was closely associated with the political and economic conditions in India.

The social climate of Bengal during the first half of the nineteenth century was powerfully conditioned by the rise of the middle classes, the spread of English education and the consequent impact of Western ideas and culture, the growth of the press, a resuscitation of the Hindu religion and the change of religious and moral values, brought about by the reforms of William Bentick and the teachings of Raja Rammohan Roy and the emphasis on rationalistic view of life, contributing to the rise of individualism. The social conditions set the stage for the emergence of the novel, a new literary form in India.[13] "Like the birth of prose, the birth of the novel too was destined to take place in Bengal and it took place in the Bengali language earlier than in any other Indian language."[14]

2.4 The Development and Growth of the Indian English Novel

As it has been mentioned earlier, the first Indian who wrote Indian English novel was Bankim Chandra Chatterjee (1838-1894). His first novel in English, *Rajmohan's Wife*, was published in 1864 and it was an experimentation with the technique of the novel form.[15]

The rest of the novels written by Indians in the later part of the nineteenth century can also be regarded as experiments with the English language. It was characteristic of the period that several of the authors were women like Toru Dutt (1856-1877) from Calcutta and Krupabai Sattianandhan (1861-1894) from Madras.[16] Indian English fiction writers of this period felt that they were writing in a prestigious language and they turned to a western audience for readership.

A period of Historical Romances followed, emphasizing the sentimental and the exotic elements. A look at some of the titles of this period illustrates this point: *Padmini: An Indian Romance* (1903) and *The Dive for Death: An Indian Romance* (1912) by T. Ramakrishna; *The Slave Girl of Agra: An Indian Historical Romance* (1909) by Romesh Chunder Dutt; *The Love of Kusuma: An Eastern Love* (1910) by Bal Krishna; *Baladitya: A Historical Romance of Ancient India* (1920) by A.S.P. Ayyar. The influence of Walter Scott could be traced in these novels which appealed to the curiosity of the Western readers about exotic India, a subject that had become the main feature of the Anglo-Indian books.[17] The Indian writers felt that they had the advantage as 'insiders' to speak about India.[18] The contribution of A. Madhaviah in South India with his novels *Thillai Govindan, Clarinda* and *Satyananda* (1909) in this regard cannot be ignored.

Another favourite subject with Indian English fiction writers of this period is the presentation of the peasantry, honest and simple.

K.S. Venkataramani is the best known writer of rural India of this period. His two novels, *Murugan, the Tiller* (1926) and *Kandan, the Patriot* (1934) describe rural life with some melancholy as it is threatened by modernity. These books deal with the portrayal of rural India to show the Indian mentality and consciousness.[19] The presentation has an insider's perception of India unlike the Anglo-Indian novel where India was seen from the outside and regarded as fundamentally unintelligible by authors like Kipling and Forster. Graham Greene, in his Introduction to *The Bachelor of Arts* of R.K. Narayan, observes: "Kipling romanticises the Indian as much as he romanticises the administrators of the Empire. E.M. Forster was funny and tender about his friend, the Maharajah of Dewas and severly ironic about the English in India, but India escaped him all the same. He wrote in *A Passage to India*: "I tried to show that India is an unexplainable muddle by introducing an unexplainable muddle. No one could find a second home in Kipling's or Forster's India."[20] The Indian English novelist wanted to show the reader the way to the Indian "Soul."

The political and social events of the thirties and forties saw the advent of Gandhi. The nationalist movement and social reforms concerned the whole of India. The independence of India became a unifying force to all kinds of nationalist, social and religious movements. "The English language seemed to have some unifying effect as it was the only pan-Indian language used by the leading men of India who represented the spirit and culture of their country, like Gandhi, Tagore, Aurobindo, Radhakrishnan, Nehru, etc."[21]

The decades of the thirties and the forties were indeed a blooming period for the Indian English fiction. A new literary movement with more peculiarly Indian features is seen emerging in the three writers who are still writing and who are still regarded as the most important Indian English novelists: R.K. Narayan with *Swami and His Friends* (1935), Mulk Raj Anand with *Untouchable* (1935) and Raja Rao with *Kanthapura* (1938). All the three novels were published in London.[22] Each novelist brought his own peculiar contribution to the Indian English novel. Mulk Raj Anand brought in the trend of social realism and humanism by championing the cause of the underprivileged.[23] R.K. Narayan sought to deal almost exclusively with the lower middle-class families of Southern India, situated in the imaginary town of Malgudi, with gentle and sympathetic irony in a tragi-comic mode whereas Raja Rao dwelt on the puranic Harikatha tradition of story-telling and made an old village woman unfold the narrative in an autobiographical form.[24] "It was in the 1930s that the Indians began what has now turned out to be their very substantial contribution on the novel in English and one peculiarly suited to their talents."[25]

After India's independence, there was a concern on the part of the novelists to choose themes and situations to present "the real India." They are very often narratives of the actual events such as the struggle for independence and its violent aftermath in the communal riots between Muslims and Hindus[26]; the terrible famine that affected the entire Bengal,[27] presentations of the timeless India in the novels of Sudhin Ghose where reality is interwoven with Indian myths[28]; the impact of Gandhi on the life of India could be seen in the number of novels published before and after independence.[29]

There are other novels that describe social changes such as the advent of urbanization affecting rural India[30]; the disintegration of the extended family in a rural or Muslim or matriarchal environment[31]; and the fight of the craftsman against the machine.[32]

Another favourite subject treated by the Indian English novelists is the encounter and confrontation between the East and West. This conflict is depicted in the following ways: love or marriage between a man and a woman of two different cultures[33]; the consequences of having returned from the West and the feeling of being alienated from one's own native culture[34]; the uncompromising attitude in politics[35] or on the level of art;[36] the feeling of rootlessness experienced by Indians when they live in another cultural environment[37]; the Eastern values from tradition and heritage are undisputed and glorified at the expense of the present time.[38] It is obvious that the conflict of cultures is an attractive and challenging subject to the Indian English novelists since many of the novelists themselves belonging to the upper social classes, have faced this conflict. The novelists who seem to be most interested in this theme are those who have left India and are living abroad such as Raja Rao, Kamala Markandaya, Balachandra Rajan, Santha Rama Rau and Attia Hosain. These novelists are expressing through their novels, a feeling of alienation and isolation, a crisis of identity, a nostalgic longing for the customs, the religion and ethos of India.

There are also novels written during this period that appeal directly to the reader's taste for exotic and sensational adventures. Manohar Malgonkar mixes adventure with politics glorifying heroism and prowess more often on the English than on the Indian side.[39] The Maharaja and the princely classes with their palace intrigues are also a favourite subject.[40] The "Saffron Robe" and the role of the "Guru" whether he is a genuine one or a charlatan, fascinate the novelists of the Indian English fiction.[41]

Today's younger writers such as Anita Desai and Arun Joshi reflect a new psychological venture. They seem to focus more on world-wide themes like isolation and rootlessness.[42]

Meenakshi Mukherjee sums up the development and growth of the Indian novel in English: "The full development of the Indian novel in English as a whole, allowing for over-simplification of details may be divided into three large stages: (1) Historical Romance (2) Social or political realism (3) Psychological novels showing introspective concern with the individual."[43] The classification of Meenakshi Mukherjee, could be accepted only as a general and broad one because it does not take into account the peculiarities of the individual novelists as well as difference between South Indian and North Indian novelists.

The Extra Literary Factors: This brief survey of the Indian English novel suggests that Indian English fiction has manifested a steady evolution through the years favoured by a number of extra literary factors.[44] K.S. Ramamurti, enumerates these factors: "The popularity of the Indian English novels in the West is because of their ability to satisfy the Western curiosity about India and Indian life; the tremendous increase within India in the size of the English-educated reading public; the multiplication of English magazines and weeklies with increasing circulation potential; the increasing demand for fiction in English among the educated classes; the great academic interest shown in Indian English literature by some university departments[45] and the intellectual groups have given the writer of Indian English fiction an importance and recognition which had not been in the past."[46]

The Indian English fiction writers are facing two major difficulties: (a) the repetitive use of the pan-Indian themes such as the impact of Gandhi, the influence of a Guru, the East-West encounter, has made them look for new subjects; (b) the competition from the novels of regional literatures that are being increasingly translated into English, suggests that the Indian English novelists can no longer claim to offer the sole representation of the Indian life and mind.[47]

2.5 The Indian English Fiction: Critical Approaches

2.5.1 The Task of Criticism

The character of the Indian novel is bound to be conditioned by the regional, linguistic and cultural peculiarities of the writer and his environment. "Whatever be the language in which it is written, a novel by an Indian writer demands direct involvement in values and experiences which are valid in the Indian context."[48] Thus, the Indian novel whether in English or in any other Indian language, has an individual and distinctive quality that is Indian which calls for serious critical attention: "A novel written by an Indian writer will certainly be Indian without any conscious effort on the part of the writer, to the extent to which he depicts Indian life and culture. . . . It can be peculiarly Indian in respect of its form, narrative techniques employed and the manner in which it adapts the English language to the native sensibility. It can be much more characteristically Indian in its moral and spiritual content and in the values and ideals it upholds, a predilection for myth and fantasy deriving from the Indian writer's unconscious affiliation with the world of legends, fables and puranas. But any deliberate attempt made by the writer to make his novel Indian or to design it for a Western audience will make it artificial and unreal."[49]

Criticism regarding the Indian novel in English has a double task: (a) It has to assess and evaluate a novel as a novel in terms of the criteria applicable to all novels whether Indian or European and in terms of universal literary values. (b) It has to elicit an aesthetic responsiveness to the distinctive Indian quality as an Indian English novel. Both these objectives had to be kept together in a delicate balance.

Both creative writing and criticism are still in the experimental stage in the realm of Indian writing in English. Neither the writer nor the critic is sure of what he should expect from the other. As a result, we have very little criticism that is objective and purposeful, oscillating between the extremes of enthusiastic approval and unbalanced veneration[50] to condemnation and complete rejection.[51] Thus, the criticism of the Indian English literature and Indian English fiction in particular tends to be experimental.[52]

2.5.2. The Critical Approaches

When we look at the criticism of the Indian English novel, the approaches taken during the last fifty years could be broadly classified thus:

(i) The Historical-Biographical Approach
(ii) The Thematic Approach
(iii) The Indian "Aesthetic" Approach
(iv) The "Formalistic" Approach
(v) The Sociological and Cultural Approach

(i) The Historical-Biographical Approach

In this approach, the critics of the Indian English fiction recount chronologically the authors and their works without much critical analysis. The division of the historical periods coincide with the social and religious movements in India during the nineteenth century and the twentieth century. The approach is "expository in character, encyclopedic in range"[53] and at times over-generous in its praise of the Indian English fiction writers. The chief among the Indian critics who take this approach are the following: K.R. Srinivasa Iyengar,[54] M.K. Naik,[55] P.P. Mehta[56] and Harish Raizada.[57]

There are also western critics who have attempted a similar approach in their writings: Ellina J. Kalinikova,[58] Haydn Moore Williams,[59] S.C. Harrex,[60] and Stephen Hemenway.[61]

The benefit of this approach is that it created a new awareness of the value and growing importance of the Indian English literature and also gave the Indian English creative writer an assurance and recognition that were not before.

The obvious question about these critics who follow the Historical-Biographical approach is whether their critical writing is sufficiently objective and well-balanced.[62] But there are a variety of extra literary considerations which make unbiased, objective evaluations difficult. "Critics are too near in time to the writers and the criticism tends to be too inductive and interpretative, too much mixed up with the biographical, social and national background of a work to make sound value judgments possible."[63]

(ii) The Thematic Approach

The thematic approach to Indian English fiction aims at identifying pan-Indian themes in the Indian English novelists. "The Indo-Anglian novelist has sometimes attempted to solve the problem of heterogeneous audience by choosing themes and situations that have more or less the same validity all over the country."[64]

In her book, *The Twice-Born Fiction*, Meenakshi Mukherjee has attempted to point out some common themes in the Indian English novelists. She suggests that the pan-Indian themes that form the basic underlying pattern in many of the Indian English novels are the following: the theme of social change, i.e. the disintegration of the old hierarchical and agrarian society and the break-down of the large joint family; the national movement for political independence and the advent of Gandhi; the encounter between the East and West not only at the level of people but also at the level of ideas[65]; the place of faith in the socio-cultural life of India, adherence to rituals and a simple faith in the superior wisdom of a Guru shaping the action and conduct of many in all parts of the country[66]; the conscious use of myths and the Indian epics which form an integral part of the nation's culture, to enhance the effect of the contemporary situation.[67] There are other Indian and Western critics who have taken this thematic approach to the Indian English novel such as Samares C. Sanyal,[68] N. Radhakrishnan,[69] G.P. Sharma,[70] Dieter Riemenschneider,[71] Klaus Steinworth[72] and S.C. Harrex.[73]

The thematic approach to the Indian English fiction asserts and affirms the traditionally multi-cultural make-up of the Indian ethos and the basic pattern familiar equally to all Indians. The discussion of the themes is highly generalized. By suggesting these generalized themes, the critics try to relate the novelists and their fiction works to India. The themes are not common to all the authors. Besides, these recognizable pan-Indian themes are not many in number and hence the novelists seem to be repetitive.[74]

This approach to the Indian English novel is not able to articulate and depict the great deal of regional variation, special and distinctive to each region of India in social structure, values, customs and problems.

(iii) The Indian "Aesthetic" Approach

The word "Aesthetic" comes from the Greek word *Aisthetikos*, perceptive by feeling. The most appropriate meaning for our discussion here from the literary point of view is "the theory of fine arts and of people's responses to them; the science or that branch of philosophy which deals with the beautiful; the doctrines of taste."[75] Among the variety of meanings given by the Oxford English dictionary (unabridged), the second meaning is the most applicable one for our discussion: "pertaining to the appreciation or criticism of the beautiful; the philosophy or theory of taste or of the perception of the beautiful in nature and art."[76]

The critics and novelists who try to explain their own understanding of the 'novel' form in the Indian literary context, are trying to formulate an Indian 'aesthetic' approach in the sense of developing a theory of art and the doctrines of taste with regard to the Indian English fiction. They attempt to articulate this approach in the following three ways:

(a) To ascertain the "Indianness"[77] "Indian sensibility"[78] in the Indian English novels.
(b) To develop an Indian criteria of evaluation of the Indian English novels using the theories of Indian poetics like the Rasa and the Dhvani as the frame of reference.
(c) Developing an Indian conception of the 'novel' form itself.

(iii) (a) Discovering the 'Indianness'

To ascertain the "Indianness" means to study the Indian English novels from "the sum total of all that is reflected in the mode of life of the Indian people and their needs, aims and aspirations."[79] The critics who have attempted to study the novels from this perspective are C.D. Narasimhaiah, Paul Verghese, P. Lal and William Walsh.

C.D. Narasimhaiah, the editor of *The Literary Criterion*, has insisted on this dimension by his critical comments on Raja Rao's work especially *The Serpent and the Rope.*[80] He highlights the use of the ancient Indian tradition, the myths and the epics and their echoes and reflections in modern Indian English writing and the process of the Indian English writers "to discover as well as to create their own identity."[81]

Paul Verghese attempts to define the concept of 'Indianness': "the sum total of cultural patterns of India and the deep seated ideas and ideals political, economic, secular and spiritual—that constitute the mind of India."[82] He emphasizes the need for the critic to make it his criteria for the analysis of Indian English fiction.

William Walsh, a sympathetic critic of Indian English literature who has popularized the Indian English writing in England discusses the Indian sensibility. He defines sensibility to be: "a special combination of thought, feeling, value and assumption, that particular taste and sentiment, that characteristic mode of action which reveal the nuance and crystallize the tone and temper of literature."[83] He analyses the Indian sensibility in Indian English novelists such as Raja Rao, R.K. Narayan, Mulk Raj Anand and poets like Nizzim Ezekiel, R. Parthasarathy and A.K. Ramanujan and concludes: "In these poets as in the novelists who preceded them . . . we see realized in the English language, the power of Indian heritage, the complexity of the Indian experience and the uniqueness of the Indian voice. We see an Eastern sensibility wholly at home in a Western Art."[84]

P. Lal, the editor of the Writers Workshop Miscellany, Calcutta has made a bold assertion that Indian English novelists are deeply rooted in the Indian tradition whose values they have discovered and constantly employ.[85] According to this viewpoint, the criterion for evaluating the Indian English fiction writers would be "Indianness": "a truly Indian work would be the one which is about India or Indians, presents an Indian point of view and has a style which fits well into the matrix of the Indian culture and way of life."[86] The above definition of the concepts of Indianness is a typical example of the serious problem involved in defining accurately the concept: a word cannot be defined by the same word. Hence the obvious problem that we encounter in making "Indianness," the criterion to judge the works of Indian English novelists is that the concept of Indianness itself is vague, nebulous and not easily definable as it has been discussed in the first part of the book. Balachancha Rajan, the novelist and critic, feels that the criterion of "Indianness" is not easy to define and the Indian English novelist, by his very profession, participates in two cultures: the Indian culture and ethos (subject-matter and content of the novel) and the Western tradition of novel writing (the form of the novel).[87]

iii (b) Theories of Indian Poetics

Closely linked to the aspect of discovering the "Indianness" of the Indian English novels, there have been efforts to develop an Indian criteria of evaluation using the theories of Indian poetics such as *Rasa* and *Dhvani* as the frame of reference.[88] "According to the *dhvani/rasa* school of poetics which has dominated Sanskrit criticism since the ninth century A.D., the soul of poetry is *rasa*, a sentiment or the essence of an emotion and this is communicated through *dhvani* suggestion or nuance."[89] These critics suggest that the *Dhvani* theory in a modern version is capable of providing a critical framework which being derived from Sanskrit sources could identify what Indian English literature owes to its roots in Indian culture and what it shares with other Indian literatures.[90]

The need for the critic to have the traditional critical standards of judgment as his frame of reference is advocated by C.D. Narasimhaiah.[91] Krishna Rayan justifies such a need as something natural to the Indian English literary critics: "The Chicago critics had their theoretical base in Aristotle's *Poetics*, the Archetypalists had theirs in Frazer's *The Golden Bough* and Jung's *Psychology of the Unconscious* and the structuralists found one in Sausser's *Course in General Linguistics*. If Indian English critics to-day feel that they would like to possess a theoretical framework, they could as these other schools have done, use an existing authoritative formulation as a source or as a point of departure. Obviously, an Indian classic of literary theory would prima facie be a good choice. A seminal work of this kind is, as we all know, the 9th century Sanskrit treatise *Dhvanyaloka* by Ananda Vardhana which sets out the theory of *dhvani*."[92]

The attempts to formulate an Indian criteria of evaluation based on the theories of Indian poetics such as *Rasa* and *Dhvani* for the Indian English literature is at a preliminary stage of clarifying concepts like *Rasa* and *Dhvani*.[93] There is a substantial speculation on the part of some Indian critics to spell out a detailed framework, eventually. But there are other critics who consider this whole attempt futile and irrelevant. Vasant A. Shahane is one of them. While discussing the important critical approaches to Indian English literature, he remarks: "Populism is peculiarly mixed up with a genuine desire to develop what are called native Indian criteria to judge the Indian English literature. The argument that we should not apply 'foreign' or 'borrowed' critical approaches to Indo-English writing and we should evolve our own 'native' 'classical' modes of criticism smacks of fake patriotism which is totally divorced from the basic requirements of such an endeavour. . . . Equally baseless and unwise is the argument that we should abjure all western modes of criticism and that we should somehow try to evolve new variants of Indian aesthetics—such as perhaps a modern *rasa* theory to understand and evaluate Indo-English writing since they are rooted in our tradition."[94]

The awareness to have an Indian criteria and the desire to develop the same to evaluate Indian English literature among the critics is commendable. It is only at an infant stage and the application of the theories of *Dhvani* and *Rasa* has yet to be tried on individual authors and their works.

iii (c) The Conception of the Indian Novel in English

The third aspect of the "aesthetic" approach to the Indian English novel is the attempt of a few Indian English novelists to voice forth their own conception of the 'novel' form.[95] The three novelists whom I would like to discuss here in this connection are Mulk Raj Anand, Raja Rao and R.K. Narayan.

Mulk Raj Anand maintains: "The novel should interpret the truth of life, from felt experience and not from books. . . . I felt that only in fiction, which is the transformation through the imagination, of the concrete life, in words, sounds and vibrations, one may probe into the many layers of human consciousness and its various phases. . . . The novel form is inevitably somewhat amorphous because it touches life into the many layers of human life."[96] The authenticity of the novel for Mulk Raj Anand is the felt experience of the novelist. "If the ultimate purpose of the novelist is to understand man, to intensify his emotions, to arouse his consciousness and to create the conditions for the experience of *rasa* or flavour or beauty, then his total consciousness, including all his faculties and experience are likely to be involved in the creative process."[97]

To have this felt experience and to see people as they were, growing in this world, Mulk Raj Anand had to search for humanness: "My searches have led me to roam round the world. And I have written in the rough ballad rhythms of an Indian English[98] in which there are inevitable echoes of the mother-tongue, about the agony of aloneness of people, in the depth of degradation in wretchedness beyond wretchedness, forced upon human beings by other human beings . . . I had to soak myself in the lives of men and women from within their tormented senses; I immersed myself in the sub world of the poor, the insulted and the injured, through continuous pilgrimages to the village, the small towns and the big town bastis of our country."[99] The novel in the hands of Anand becomes " a creative weapon for attaining humanness."[100]

Raja Rao conceives of literature itself as *Sadhana* a spiritual experience "to be in contact with the ultimate reality."[101] He expresses this conception of literature in the following words: "Literature as *Sadhana* is the best life for a writer. The Indian tradition which links the word with the absolute *Sabdabrahman* has clearly shown the various ways by which one can approach literature, without the confusions that arise in the mind of the western writer viewing life as an intellectual adventure. Basically an Indian outlook follows a deeply satisfying, richly rewarding and profoundly metaphysical path."[102] In this quest for the ultimate truth, the novelist becomes a *Sadhaka* which means the one who devotes himself with singular devotion and dedication to the quest for the ultimate knowledge that lies hidden beneath the veil of appearance.[103] "The best thing would be to call me a *Sadhaka* . . . one who tries to live what he believes to be true is the *Sadhaka*. It is very difficult to find a parallel word in English."[104]

Raja Rao maps out the process of his quest for the ultimate through the novel form and explores the possibilities of being and becoming. He spells out his idea of the novel clearly in his interview with Shiva Niranjan on March 15, 1978, in New Delhi to this specific question:

> Shiva Niranjan: What is your aesthetic of the novel? How far is it a departure from the western conception of a well-made novel?
>
> Raja Rao: The aesthetic is that, sometimes, I like to write like a *purana*. I like the puranic conception. That is the only conception of novel for me. I don't want to compare my novel with any foreign novel. . . . I am very much an Indian and the Indian form is the puranic form.[105]
> The novel is conceived as a purana "an interminable tale."[106]

Thus, Raja Rao attempts to formulate an Indian conception of the novel:

"The Indian novel can only be epic in form and metaphysical in nature. It can only be a story within a story to show all stories are parables."[107] Raja Rao has followed this conception of the novel and the technique in his novels from *The Serpent and the Rope.*

This Indian approach to the novel is questioned and examined by critics like David McCutchion in his review article "Novel as *Shastra*" where he discusses *The Serpent and the Rope* and raises the following questions: "Is this a novel at all? Is it not rather a book of wisdom, a compendium of interminable commentary and philosophising where even the conversations are dialogues in pursuit of truth—a book of discursive enquiry rather than narration."[108] A discerning reader of the novel *The Serpent and the Rope* is justified in asking these questions.

R.K. Narayan has not spelt out clearly his conception of the Indian novel in English. One could glean from his interviews and essays, the idea he has of the Indian novel in English. He considers: "Literature is not a branch of study to be placed in a separate compartment for the edification only of scholars but a comprehensive and artistic medium of expression to benefit the literate and illiterate alike."[109]

The two requisites needed for an Indian novel in English according to R.K. Narayan are his direct and immediate contact with the subject or persons he is writing about and an immersion into the myths and legends of India. R.K. Narayan insists on the story-telling aspect of the novel resembling the myths and legends of India. "The novelist is certainly not a social reformer. He is a story-teller, a raconteur, repeating the work of the gods in idly making and dissolving endless spheres for mere amusement of the process itself for diversion, entertainment, play (*Lila*)."[110] To be a good story-teller, the novelist should feel within his bones, the immediacy of the subject he is writing about: "The impact of life is direct and you have to express yourself in a very direct manner."[111] Narayan believes that India is rich in material for the novelist if only he has the perceptive eye to observe it.[112]

The second important requisite for an Indian novelist in English according to R.K. Narayan is his immersion into the rich religious traditions of India especially its myths and legends. "To be a good writer anywhere, you must have roots both in religion and in family. I have these things."[113] Narayan's complete familiarity with the Hindu myths and legends and his easy intimacy with the *Ramayana* and the *Mahabharata* manifested in his novels, shows him to be deeply rooted in Indian culture and justifies his expectation of the Indian English novelist to be at home with the rich religious tradition of India. Evidences to this fact will be given in a latter part of the book. William Walsh testifies to this fact in the following words: "The truth is that the Hindu myths and religious parables . . . sink deep into the constitution of the novelist. These things are present and influential not as dogma or metaphysics but as part of a mode of perception and a habit of reaction. They flow in and out of the writer's thought and touch. The religious sense of Indian myth is part of Narayan's grip of reality, of his particular view of human life and his individual way of placing and ordering human feeling and experience."[114]

The attempts of Mulk Raj Anand, Raja Rao and R.K.Narayan to formulate a conception of the Indian novel in English insist upon the felt experience of the novelist, the immediate and direct contact with the Indian experience, the immersion into the myths and legends of India, the spiritual experience of the novelist of the ultimate truth. This could also be called 'the empirical approach.' The value and significance of these attempts are that they point to a direction to the future to have an Indian conception of the 'novel' form.

(iv) The "Formalistic" Approach

The word 'Form' is used in different meanings. The meaning that is most suitable for our discussion here is: "The style of expressing the thoughts and ideas in literary or musical composition, including the arrangement and order of the different parts of the whole. Also, method of arranging the ideas in logical reasoning; good or just order of ideas and logical sequence."[115] *The Webster's Dictionary* also gives the same meaning distinguishing "form" from content: "arrangement, especially orderly arrangement; way that something is put together; pattern, style, distinguished from content."[116]

The word "Form" is used in the sense of arrangement especially orderly arrangement, shape and structure of the novel by the critics who use the 'Formalistic' approach to the Indian English fiction. The critics are only a handful. "The search for 'form' or the attempt to find the key to the structure and the meaning of a work of art or to discover its 'shape' or to fathom its effect or how it has come about these roads are not taken by critics yet."[117] Vasant Shahane makes an attempt to examine 'the form' in Indian English fiction. The meaning he gives to the word 'Form' is "the shape or structure of the novel"[118] and he ascertains: "The question of form in Indian Writing in English fiction suffers from two drawbacks. The first failing may be simply described as 'no form.' . . . the non-existence of form. . . . The second drawback is the 'wrong form.' This wrong form betrays a lack of cohesiveness in a novel. Its failure to hold together its sprawling elements and its failing as an art entity."[119]

These are sweeping generalizations without sufficient evidence or proof. Shahane refers also to the attempts to understand the 'form' in Indian English fiction by Raja Rao, and Meenakshi Mukherjee[121] in her book *The Twice-Born Fiction.* As we can see, the discussion on 'Form' in Indian English fiction is still at a preliminary stage.

In addition to this analysis of the 'Form' i.e. the structure of the novel, is the examination of the style of the Indian English novelists and their use of the English language. The critics at best are able to point out the peculiarities of the use of the English language by the different novelists and the influence of the native tongues in the use of English by the Indian English novelists. Ramesh Mohan[122] and David McCutchion[123] are some of the important critics who are interested in this aspect of the criticism of the Indian English fiction.

(v) The Sociological and Cultural Approach

The sociological and cultural approach considers the Indian English novels as documents and sources of cultural knowledge about India. "Indo-Anglian fiction is a major source for a systematic study of cultural contact and cultural change with the Indian world-view as a focus of the Westerners, to increase their knowledge of acculturation processes."[124] Dorothy M. Spenser, as a Professor of Anthropology at the Institute of South Asian Regional Studies, University of Pennsylvania, was one of the earliest critics who published a comprehensive bibliography of Indian fiction in English. She maintains the fact that western readers are interested in Indian English novels because they regard them as a valuable source of information about India. She comments on the novels according to the value they have for sociologists and anthropologists.[125] The other critics who follow this trend of criticism of the Indian English novels is M.E. Derrett[126] and Kai Nicholson.[127]

In this approach, the function of literature as a mirror of society is taken for granted. None of these critics pay any attention to style, the narrator's point of view and the literary tradition. It is significant to note that only the Western critics have used the Indian English novels as sources of cultural knowledge.

In short, we can sum up some of the critical approaches taken to study the Indian English fiction are as follows; the historical-biographical, the thematic, the Indian "aesthetic" approach, the "formalistic" approach that includes the linguistic aspect of the novels and the sociological and cultural approach where the novels serve as documents of cultural knowledge.

2.6 Introducing the Present Study

The study that is undertaken in this book is an extension as well as focusing and sharpening of the cultural approach to Indian English fiction, restricting it to the South Indian novelists in English to highlight the regional element. The discovery of the strong regional and cultural element liberates the concept of 'Indianness' from its vagueness and makes it manageable, concrete and existential. The reason for selecting the South Indian novelists is to situate them in their cultural milieu and to sharpen the cultural study of the novels. The South Indian novelists are studied not out of curiosity but they are analysed in order to identify the peculiar and the distinctive South Indian cultural values and assumptions. The elaboration and explication of this approach and the meaning and definition of the terms: culture, values, assumptions, South Indian novelists in English, the reason for the selection of these authors will be attempted in the next part.

NOTES

1. Klaus Steinworth, *The Indo-English Novel* (Wiesbaden: Franz Steiner Verlag, 1975), p. 4.
2. *Ibid.*
3. Hari Mohan Prasad, ed., *Indian English Novelists* (New Delhi: Sterling, 1982).
4. K.S. Ramamurti, *Rise of the Indian Novel in English* (New Delhi: Sterling, 1987), p. 2.
5. *Ibid.*, p. 38.
6. *Ibid.*, p. 40.
7. *Ibid.*, p. 42.
8. A detailed treatment of this aspect could be found in the following books: John B. Alphonso-Karkala, *Indo-English Literature in the Nineteenth Century* (Mysore: University of Mysore, 1970), pp. 6-33.
9. Paul Verghese, *Problems of the Indian Creative Writer in English* (Bombay: Somaiya, 1971), pp. 2-4.
10. M.K. Naik, *A History of Indian English Literature* (New Delhi: Sahitya Akademi, 1982), p. 4.
11. K.S. Ramamurti, *Rise of the Indian Novel in English*, p. 35.
12. *Ibid.*
13. *Ibid.*, p. 34.
14. *Ibid.*, p. 35.
15. Klaus Steinworth, *The Indo-English Novel*, p. 3.

16. *Ibid.*, p. 4.
17. The books that are referred to here are E.M. Forster, *The Passage to India* (1924), Rudyard Kipling, *Kim* (1901).
18. M.E. Derrett, *The Modern Indian Novel in English* (Brussels: Editions de l'Instititutede Sociologie, Universite' Libre de Bruxelles, 1966), p. 17.
19. Klaus Steinworth, p. 5.
20. Graham Greene, "Introduction," *The Bachelor of Arts*, R.K.Narayan, (Chicago: University of Chicago Press, 1980), pp. v-vi.
21. Klaus Steinworth, p. 5.
22. *Ibid.*
23. The very titles of Anand's first novels illustrate this point: *Untouchable* (1935), *Coolie* (1936).
24. Shyam M. Asnani, "The Socio-Political Scene of the 1930s: Its Impact on the Indo-English Novel," *Commonwealth Quarterly*, 6, 21 (December 1981), p. 18.
25. William Walsh, "The Indian Sensibility in English," *Awakened Conscience*, ed. C.D. Narasimhaiah (New Delhi: Sterling, 1978), p. 66.
26. Khushwant Singh, *Train to Pakistan* (1956); K.A. Abbas, *Inquilab* (1955); Chaman Nahal, *Azadi* (1975).
27. Bhabani Bhattacharya, *So Many Hungers* (1947).
28. The tetralogy of Sudhin Ghose, *Gazelles Leaping* (1949); *Cradle of the Clouds* (1951); *The Vermillion Boat* (1953); *The Flame of the Forest* (1955).
29. The significant works of fiction inspired by Gandhi and dealing with the theme of freedom struggle are K.S. Venkataramani, *Kandan, the Patriot* (1932); Frieda H. Das, *Into the Sun* (1933); Mulk Raj Anand, *Untouchable* (1935); Raja Rao, *Kanthapura* (1938); D.F. Karaka, *We Never Die* (1944); Amir Ali, *Conflict* (1947); R.K. Narayan, *Waiting for the Mahatma* (1955); Nayantara Sahgal, *A Time to be Happy* (1955); Kamala Markandaya, *Some Inner Fury* (1955); Khushwant Singh, *I Shall Not Hear the Nightingale* (1959); K. Nagarajan, *The Chronicles of Kedaram* (1961).
30. Kamala Markandaya, *Nectar in a Sieve* (1954), *A Handful of Rice* (1966), *Two Virgins* (1973). These three novels discuss the penetration of urbanization into very structure of rural India.
31. Mulk Raj Anand, *The Sword and the Sickle* (1942); Attia Hosain, *Sunlight on a Broken Column* (1961); Meon Marath, *Wounds of Spring* (1961).
32. Mulk Raj Anand, *The Big Heart* (1945).
33. Kamala Markandaya, *Some Inner Fury* (1955); Raja Rao, *The Serpent and the Rope* (1960).
34. Santha Rama Rau, *Remember the House* (1956); Balachandra Rajan, *The Dark Dancer* (1958).
35. Nayantara Sahgal, *This Time of Morning* (1965).
36. Kamala Markandaya, *Possession* (1963).
37. Kamala Markandaya, *The Nowhere Man* (1972).

38. Attia Hosain, *Sunlight on a Broken Column* (1961).
39. Manohar Malgonkar, *Distant Drum* (1960), *Combat of Shadows* (1962), *A Bend in the Ganges* (1964).
40. Mulk Raj Anand, *Private Life of an Indian Prince* (1953) and Manohar Malgonkar, *The Princes* (1963).
41. R.K. Narayan, *The Guide* (1958); Nergis Dalal, *The Inner Door* (1975); Bhabani Bhattacharya, *He Who Rides a Tiger* (1960); Sudhin Ghose, *The Flame of the Forest* (1955); Kamala Markandaya, *A Silence of Desire* (1960); *Possession* (1963); G.V.Desani. *All About H. Hatterr* (1948).
42. Anita Desai, *Cry, the Peacock* (1963), *Voices in the City* (1965), *Bye, Bye, Blackbird* (1971), *Where Shall We Go This Summer* (1975), *Fire on the Mountain* (1977), *Clear Light of Day* (1980) *In Custody* (1985). Arun Joshi, *The Foreigner* (1968), *The Strange Case of Billy Biswas* (1971), *The Apprentice* (1974), *The Last Labyrinth* (1981).
43. Meenakshi Mukherjee, *The Twice-Born Fiction* (New Delhi: Arnold Heinemann, 1971), p. 19.
44. K.S. Ramamurti, *Rise of the Indian Novel in English*, p. 7.
45. Meenakshi Mukherjee, "Over Kill: The State of Research in Indo-Anglian Fiction," *Journal of Literary Studies,* 2, 2 (December 1979), pp. 1-2.
46. K.S. Ramamurti, p. 8.
47. Klaus Steinworth, p. 8.
48. Meenakshi Mukherjee, p. 19.
49. K.S. Ramamurti, p. 4.
50. Srinivasa Iyengar, *Indian Writing in English* (New Delhi: Sterling, 1983), p. 6.
51. T.V. Subba Rao, *Indian Writing in English: Is There Any Worth in it?* (Madurai: Koodal Publishers, 1976), p. 24.
52. Srinivasa Iyengar, p. 21.
53. Vasant A. Shahane, "Indo-English Literature: Its Major Concerns and Its Academic Rationale," *Alien Voice: Perspectives on Commonwealth Literature,* p. 16.
54. Srinivasa Iyengar, *Indian Writing in English,* 1983.
55. M.K. Naik, *A History of Indian English Literature*, 1982.
56. P.P. Mehta, *Indo-Anglian Fiction: An Assessment* (Bareilly: Prakash, 1968).
57. Harish Raizada, *The Lotus and the Rose: Indian Fiction in English, 1857-1947* (Aligarh: Muslim University, 1978; New Delhi: Young India, 1978).
58. Ellina Kalinikova, *Indian English Literature: A Perspective* (Ghaziabad: Vimal, 1982).
59. Haydn Moore Williams, *Indo-Anglian Literature: 1800-1970: A Survey,* (Madras: Orient Longman, 1976). Haydn Moore Williams, *Studies in Modern Indian Fiction in English* (Calcutta: Writers Workshop Miscellany Publication, 1973).
60. S.C. Harrex, *The Modern Novel in English* (Calcutta: Writers Workshop,

1971).

61. Stephen Hemenway, *The Novel of India,* (Calcutta: Writers Workshop, 1975) Vol II.
62. Meenakshi Mukherjee, p. 11,
63. K.S. Ramamurti, p. 11.
64. Meenakshi Mukherjee, p. 25.
65. *Ibid.*, p. 27.
66. *Ibid.*, p. 29.
67. *Ibid.*, p. 31.
68. Samares C. Sanyal, *Indianness in Major Indo-English Novels* (Bareilly: Prakash, 1984).
69. N. Radhakrishnan, *Indo-Anglian Fiction: Major Trends and Themes* (Madras: Emerald, 1984).
70. G.P. Sharma, *Nationalism in Indo-Anglian Fiction* (Delhi: Sterling, 1978).
71. Dieter Riemenschneider, "The Indo-English Novel," *Indian Literature,* (September-October 1983), pp. 27-39.
72. Klaus Steinworth, *The Indo-English Novel.*
73. S.C. Harrex, *The Fire and the Offering: The English Language Novel of India (1935-1970)* (Calcutta: Writers Workshop, 1978).
74. Meenakshi Mukherjee, p. 25.
75. *Webster's Dictionary of the English Language* (Unabridged, Encyclopedic edition, New York: Publishers International Press, 1977), p. 31
76. *Compact Edition of the Oxford English Dictionary* (Oxford University Press, 1971), vol. I, p. 37.
77. C.D. Narasimhaiah, "Raja Rao's *Kanthapura" Fiction and the Reading Public,* ed. C.D. Narasimhaiah (Mysore: University of Mysore, 1965), p. 78.
78. M.E. Derrett, p. 79.
79. Samares C. Sanyal, p. xii.
80. C.D. Narasimhaiah, *The Swan and the Eagle* (Simla: Indian Institute of Advanced Study, 1969), p. 199.
81. *Ibid.*, p. 18.
82. Paul Verghese, *Essays on Indian Writing in English* (New Delhi: N.V. Publishers, 1975), p. 3.
83. William Walsh, "The Indian Sensibility in English," *Awakened Conscience,* p. 62.
84. *Ibid.*, p. 71.
85. P. Lal, *The Concept of Indian Literature* (Calcutta: Writers Workshop, 1968). The whole book argues this point.
86. R.S. Pathak, "The Indo-English Novelist's Quest for Identity," *Explorations in Modern Indo-English Fiction,* ed. R.K. Dhawan (New Delhi: Bahri, 1983), p. 2.
87. Balachandra Rajan, "Identity and Nationality," *Commonwealth Literature: Unity and Diversity in a Common Culture,* ed. John Press

(London: Heinemann Educational Books, 1965), p. 106.

88. Ragini Ramachandra, "A Report on the Proceedings of the Seminar on 'Towards the Formulation of a Common Poetic for Indian Literature To-Day' held at Dhvanyaloka, Mysore from January 26th to 28th, 1984." *Literary Criterion,* 19, 1 (1984), pp. 66-81.
89. Roshni Rustomji, "Rasa and Dhvani in Indian and Western Poetics and Poetry," *Journal of South Asian Literature,* 16, 1 (Winter-Spring 1981), p. 75. A.L. Basham, *The Wonder That Was India* (London: Sidgwick and Jackson, 1954), p. 417.
90. Krishna Rayan, "Towards an Indian Critical Tradition for Indian Writing in English," *Indian Journal of English Studies,* 25 (1985), p. 5
91. C.D. Narasimhaiah, "Search for Values in Literary Criticism: Some Major Shifts in the Indian Academic Situation," *Moving Frontiers of English Studies in India* (New Delhi: S..Chand, 1977), p. 83. C.D. Narasimhaiah, *Literary Criticism: European and Indian Tradition* (Mysore: University of Mysore, 1965). The book is devoted to the explanation and description of the concepts of *Rasa* and *Dhvani.*
92. Krishna Rayan, "Towards an Indian Critical Tradition for Indian Writing in English," p. 5.
93. Krishna Rayan, "The Case for an Indian Poetic Based on the Dhvani Theory," *Literary Criterion*, 19, 1 (1984), pp. 41-50. K. Krishnamoorthy, "Dhvani or suggestion: A Study in Perspective," *Indian Literature,* 28, 4 (July-August 1985), pp. 113-27. Roshni Rustomji, "Rasa and Dhvani in Indian and Western Poetics and Poetry," pp. 75-88.
94. Vasant A. Shahane, "Indo-English Literature: Its Major Concerns and Its Academic Rationale," *Alien Voice,* pp. 18-19.
95. One could profitably compare the literary movement of novel criticism in the West especially in British literature, that has resulted in "The Theory of the Novel."
96. Mulk Raj Anand, "Why I Write," *Indian Writing in English,* ed. K.N. Sinha (New Delhi: Heritage, 1979), pp. 6-7.
97. Mulk Raj Anand, "A Note on Modern Indian Fiction," *Indian Literature,* 8:1 (January-February 1965), p. 53.
98. Mulk Raj Anand, "Pigeon Indian: Some Notes on Indian English Writing," *World Literature Written in English*, 21, 1 (Summer 1982), pp. 325-35.
99. Mulk Raj Anand, "Why I Write," p. 8.
100. Mulk Raj Anand, "Roots and Flowers" (Two Lectures on the metamorphosis of technique and content in the Indian English novel) (Dharwar: Karnataka University, 1972), p. 36.
101. Shiva Niranjan, "An Interview with Raja Rao," *Indian Writing in English,* ed. K.N. Sinha, p. 20.
102. Harish Raizada, "Literature as 'Sadhana': The Progress of Raja Rao from *Kanthapura* to *The Serpent and the Rope*," *Indo-English Literature,* ed. K.K. Sharma (Ghaziabad: Vimal, 1977), p. 158.
103. Shiva Niranjan, *Raja Rao: Novelist as Sadhaka* (Ghaziabad: Vimal,

1977), p. 158.

104. Shiva Niranjan, "An Interview with Raja Rao," p. 26.
105. *Ibid.*, p. 20.
106. Raja Rao, "Foreword," *Kanthapura* (London: Oxford University Press, 1963).
107. Harish Raizada, "Literature as 'Sadhana,'" p. 174.
108. David McCutchion, "The Novel as Shastra," *Considerations,* ed. Meenakshi Mukherjee (New Delhi: Allied, 1977), p. 92.
109. R.K. Narayan, "The World of the Story-Teller" (an extract from the introduction of the author to his book *Gods, Demons and Others,* the stories from the *Ramayana* and the *Mahabharata*), *Fiction and the Reading Public in India,* ed. C.D. Narasimhaiah (Mysore: University of Mysore, 1967), pp. 234-35.
110. Margaret Berry, "R.K. Narayan: Lila and Literature," *The Journal of Indian Writing in English*, 4, 2 (January 1976), p. 3.
111. O.P. Saxena, *Glimpses of Indo-Anglian Fiction* (New Delhi: Jaisons, 1982), vol. I, p. 25.
112. V.Y. Kantak, "The Achievement of Narayan," *Indian Literature of the Past Fifty Years,* ed. C.D. Narasimhaiah (Mysore: University of Mysore, 1970), p. 139.
113. Ved Mehta, ed., "The Train Had Just Arrived at Malgudi Station," *The Newyorker*, 38 (15 September 1962), p. 61.
114. William Walsh, *R.K. Narayan: A Critical Appreciation* (New Delhi: Allied, 1983), p. 166.
115. *The Oxford English Dictionary*, vol. I, p. 1057.
116. *Webster's Dictionary of the English Language*, p. 720.
117. Vasant A. Shahane, "Indo-English Literature: Its Major Concerns and Its Academic Rationale," *Alien Voice,* p. 19.
118. Vasant A. Shahane, "Raja Rao's *The Cat and Shakespeare:* A Study in the Form of Fiction," *Journal of Indian Writing in English*, 3, 1 (January 1975).
119. *Journal of Indian Writing in English*, 2, 2 (July 1974), p. 35.
120. Vasant A. Shahane, "Indo-Anglian Fiction and the Question of Form," *Journal of Indian Writing in English,* 2, 2 (July 1974), p. 23.
121. *Ibid.*, p. 34.
122. Ramesh Mohan, ed., *Indian Writing in English* (New Delhi: Orient Longman, 1978).
123. David McCutchion, *Indian Writing in English: Critical Essays* (Calcutta: Writers Workshop, 1969).
124. Dorothy M. Spenser, *Indian Fiction in English: An Annotated Bibliography* (Philadelphia: University of Pennsylvania Press, 1960), p. 11.
125. *Ibid.*, p. 15.
126. M.E. Derrett, *The Modern Indian Novel in English.*
127. Kai Nicholson, *A Representation of Social Problems in the Indo-Anglian and the Anglo-Indian Novel* (Bombay: Jaico, 1972).

Part III

The Cultural Approach: The South Indian Element

3.1 Literature and Culture

Literature is an embodiment and treasury of cultural knowledge. the study of literature is one of the best ways of understanding the nuances of a culture.[1] Paul Verghese maintains rather sweepingly: "There is no better yardstick to measure the culture of a nation than her literature which is 'an expression of society.'"[2]

3.2 The Regional Element

One of the important objectives of the Indian English writers of fiction has been the creative interpretation of Indian culture and the formulation and projection of the Indian image.[3] In this context, it is useful to study selected South Indian novelists in English to highlight and identify their distinctive South Indian cultural values and assumptions. By focusing on the cultural approach to the Indian English novelists of South India we shall discover the regional element in their works and not merely pan-Indian themes, concerns and assumptions that we have discussed in the previous part of the book. This possibility is indicated by various critics who take different approaches to Indian English fiction such as Ellina J. Kalinikova, Meenakshi Mukherjee and Krishna Rayan.

Ellina J. Kalinikova, the Russian critic who uses the historical-biographical approach, affirms the presence of the regional element in the novels of R.K. Narayan: "In Narayan's creative work, a belonging to the Tamil environment is found quite easily because it is connected with the philosophy, art and culture of Tamilnadu."[4] Meenakshi Mukherjee, taking the thematic approach to Indian fiction states: "R.K. Narayan's novels are so satisfyingly Indian perhaps because they are so authentically South Indian. This means not only that he depicts customs and manners of the Tamil people accurately, but what is more important, through skilful use of the English language, he delineates people whose actions, behaviour and responses are shaped by a language different from English. . . . What R.K. Narayan does very unobtrusively, Raja Rao does more in a conspicuous way in *Kanthapura* dealing with Kannada speaking characters."[5]

Krishna Rayan, while trying to evolve an Indian critical tradition for Indian writing in English following the "aesthetic" approach of using the theories of Indian poetics observes: "To William Walsh, the ethos of Narayan's novels is Indian. But to Balachandra Rajan, it is South Indian. Narayan himself has described his personality rooted to the right triangle of Madras, Mysore and Coimbatore. . . . The details of landscape, the exterior at least of human behaviour, certain tricks of expression and at times even the speech rhythms are recognizably Tamilian, Kannadiga rather than generically Indian."[6]

Thus, several critics of Indian English fiction, whatever might be the critical approaches they undertake, have pointed out the presence of the regional element in Indian English novels. They have not elaborated the cultural approach to grasp and understand the regional element.

3.3 The Aim of the Present Study

The aim of the present study is to elaborate the cultural approach to discover and analyse, interpret and evaluate the South Indian regional and cultural element in the selected South Indian novelists in English such as R.K. Narayan, Raja Rao, Kamala Markandaya, K.R. Venkataramani, K. Nagarajan, Balachandra Rajan and Santha Rama Rau. This study will aim at analysing not merely the cultural values and assumptions from the distinctive viewpoint of being South Indian but also will explore the different ways and the emphasis with which these novelists present them.

3.4 Questions about Novel-Writing

Before we explain the various terms involved in the topic of analysis such as culture, values, assumptions, South Indian novelists in English and the reason for their selection, it will be appropriate to raise certain fundamental questions with regard to the purpose of novel-writing itself in English by the South Indian novelists: For example, to what extent is the novel used as a communication vehicle with the educated in India and the Western audience or as a means of propaganda for social, political and economic reforms? To what extent does the novel become an interpreter of the indigenous culture? How effective is the communication of the cultural affirmation of the indigenous values and feelings? How does English language itself become indigenized to reassert South

Indian cultural values? In other words, how far do the South Indian novelists in English adapt the English language to reassert the traditional cultural values?

In the South Indian novelists chosen for our study, the novels are used as a means of communication with Indians as well as western readers to give them an account of the South Indian culture and certain changes that are taking place within the traditional cultural values and assumptions. The novels also become vehicles of self-expression in which the English language itself gets integrated and adapted into the text of the novels. These issues will be discussed in detail in the following parts of the book.

3.5 The Explanation of the Terms

A. Culture

There are many definitions of culture. The aim of this section is to have a brief survey of the different views expressed by anthropologists, sociologists and literary critics on culture in order to provide a foundation for my working definition of culture. Hence, this section excludes the evaluation and examination of the merits and demerits of each of the definitions in detail proposed on culture.

(i) The Meaning of the Word

The Unabridged Oxford English Dictionary (A New English Dictionary on Historical Principles, 1961) indicates 'culture' deriving from the Latin word 'Culture' which means cultivation, tending and in Christian authors, worship the action and practice of cultivating the soil, village or husbandry; the cultivating or rearing of a plant or crop.[7] Only in its fourth meaning, the word 'culture' means the cultivating and development of the mind, faculties, manners; the improvement or refinement by education and training, the intellectual side of civilization.[8] According to *The Encyclopedia of Religion and Ethics*, the word is best understood "intensively as humanity's effort to assert its inner and independent being."[9]

(ii) Anthropologists and Sociologists

It was Edward B. Tylor, a British anthropologist who, in 1871, first gave a standard and systematic definition of culture: "Culture or civilization, taken in its wide ethnographic sense, is that complex whole which includes knowledge, belief, art, morals, law, custom and any other capabilities and habits acquired by man as a member of society. The condition of culture among the various societies of mankind, insofar as it is capable of being investigated on general principles is a subject apt for the study of laws of human thought and action."[10]

This concept of culture became a tool for analysing the social habits of tribes or ethnic groups. This is an all-embracing definition of culture and Tylor does not distinguish social organization and social institutions from a general concept of culture.[11]

Tylor's definition has been refined many times. In 1952, A.L. Krober and Clyde Kluckhohn published *Culture: A Critical Review of Concepts and Definitions.*[12] The purpose of this work was threefold: (i) To make available in one place for the purposes of reference, a collection of definitions by anthropologists, sociologists, psychologists, philosophers and others (the section on definitions offers 164 definitions. Close to three hundred definitions are included in the monograph as a whole); (ii) to document the gradual emergence and refinement of a concept that is of great significance; (iii) to assist other investigators in reaching agreement and greater precision in definition by pointing out and commenting upon agreements and disagreements in the definitions.[13] After reviewing the various definitions, Krober and Kluckhohn offer a definition of culture: "Culture consists of patterns, explicit and implicit, of and for behaviour acquired and transmitted by symbols, constituting the distinctive achievement of human groups, including their embodiments in artifacts; the essential core of culture consists of traditional (i.e. historically derived and selected) ideas and especially their attached values; culture systems may, on the one hand, be considered as products of action, on the other as conditioning elements of further action."[14]

This formulation represents a condensation of the earlier statements of the American anthropologists on culture. It is certainly a more adequate formulation than 'culture is learned behaviour,'[15] Krober and Kluckhohn observed that culture is not mere behaviour nor the investigation of behaviour. It also consists of norms for or standards of behaviour and ideologies justifying and rationalizing certain selected ways of behaviour.[16]

Other anthropologists like Melville Herskovits and George Peter Murdock try to understand the concept of culture by describing its characteristics: "Culture is learned; derives from the biological, environmental, psychological and historical components of human existence; structured; divided into aspects; dynamic, variable, exhibits regularities that permit its analysis by the methods of science; the instrument whereby the individual adjusts to his total setting and gains the means for creative expression. . . . Defined as the man-made part of the environment, culture a construct that describes that total body of belief, behaviour, knowledge, sanctions, values and goals that mark the way of life of any people . . . in the final analysis it comprises the things that people have, the things they do and what they think."[17]

George Peter Murdock maintains that all human cultures in spite of their diversity have fundamentally a great deal in common and these common aspects, he believes, can be analysed scientifically. In this context, he provides a theoretical orientation towards the study of culture, a series of seven basic assumptions: "Culture is learned. It is inculcated, social, ideational, gratifying, adaptive and integrative."[18] These are attempts to describe culture in a general way. They do not define it very precisely.

Various other definitions have been put forward by anthropologists and sociologists emphasizing some of the aspects of culture: social heritage, learned behaviour, ideas, shared or standardized behaviour, abstraction from behaviour, super-organism, symbol and meaning.

The aspect of social heritage is stressed in the definition of culture by Bronislaw Malinowski,[19] Edward Sapir,[20] Ralph Linton,[21] Robert Lowie.[22]

Definitions that emphasize culture as learned behaviour have been employed by many psychologists, sociologists and anthropologists like Ruth Benedict,[23] Julian Steward,[24] Allison Davis,[25] Kluckhohn.[26] Some other anthropologists like Clark Wissler,[27] James Ford[28] have looked at culture to be ideas shared by members of a society. There are other definitions of culture that have placed major emphasis on shared (or standardized) behaviour. Geoffrey Gores,[29] Talcott Parsons[30] and Kimball Young,[31] Krober[32] and Kluckhohn[33] and David Aberle and his companions[34] express the view that culture is an abstraction from behaviour. A.L. Krober considers culture to be "super organic and super individual."[35] The definitions of culture Leslie A. White[36] and Clifford Geertz[37] emphasize the aspects of symbol and meaning.

Tylor's omnibus definition of culture is the basis of most anthropological theories of culture. This conception has been developed in different directions as we observe from the above discussion. Two theories of culture have dominated the anthropological thinking from the beginning of the century. They are the process-pattern theory derived from Boas and best represented by Kroeber and the structural functional theory derived from Malinowski and Radcliffe-Brown. The process-pattern theory takes pattern as the basis and the structural theory takes social structure as the basis and both the theories cover the entire range of Tylor's concept.[39] There have been attempts to integrate both these dimensions of culture by such as these: Firth, Fallers, Geertz and Schneider. "If . . . society is taken to be an organized set of individuals with a given way of life, Culture is that way of life. If society is taken to be an aggregate of social relations, then culture is the content of those relations. Society emphasizes the human component, the aggregate of peoplè and the relation between them. Culture emphasizes the component of accumulated resources, immaterial as well as material, which the people inherit, employ, transmute, add to and transmit."[40] Hence culture is patterns for behaviour, the way of life of a people.

(iii) Approaches to Culture

There is an increasing awareness of the deep and intrinsic relationship between culture and life of the people. This could be seen in some of the following approaches to culture.

(a) Culture as the way of life of a people
(b) Culture as the product of a dominant class
(c) Culture as "great tradition" and "little tradition"
(d) Culture that provides a 'world-view' to people

(a) Culture is the way people live.[41] It is the way people understand themselves, organize themselves and celebrate life. Their self-understanding results in a world-view which finds expression in myths and symbols. Klinberg confirms this viewpoint: Culture as 'that whole "way of life" which is determined by social environment.[42] Culture . . . has come to mean, most simply, the entire way of life followed by a people.[43]

(b) The popularization of the social notion of culture: a dominant culture, product of a dominating class is the influence of the Marxist analysis of culture. The owners of the means of production impose their values and their culture on the sub-ordinate classes. For Karl Marx, there is a constant interplay between social classes manifested in the economic and cultural domination of the powerful over the poor. "Though all may consume cultural products, it is a privileged minority that controls the production, circulation and consumption of culture. This minority controls the machinery of legitimization and sanction."[44] In a passage in *The German Ideology,* Marx wrote: "The ideas of the dominating class are, in all epochs, dominating ideas. That means that the class which is the material dominating power in society is, at the same time, its spiritual dominating power. The class which disposes of the means of material production, disposes therefore, at the same time, of the means of intellectual production . . . the ideas of those who are deprived of the means of intellectual production are subjected to that of the dominating class."[45]

(c) In addition to the notion of dominant culture, there are also suggestions of two components of culture, such as the "great tradition" and the "little tradition" considered by social anthropologists such as Redfield Robert[46] and M.N. Srinivas in India. M.N. Srinivas explains the meaning of these two terms, "In a civilization, there is great tradition of the reflective few and there is a little tradition of the largely unreflective many. The great tradition is cultivated in schools or temples; the little tradition works itself out and keeps itself going in the lives of the unlettered in their village communities."[47]

(d) Culture provides the perceptions of reality that govern the lives of people. These perceptions of reality (man in relation to himself, man in relation to other men, man in relation to nature, man in relation to God) become conceptualizations. These conceptualizations form what is termed as the "World-view" of the culture. "The World-view is the central systematization of conceptions of reality to which the members of the culture assent (largely unconsciously) and from which stem, their value system. The World-view lies at the very heart of culture, touching, interacting with and strongly influencing every other aspect of the culture."[48] There are five major functions of this "World-view": Explanation of how and why things got to be as they are; Evaluation, the function of judging and validating the basic institutions, values and goals of a society; the function of psychological reinforcement for that particular group at crisis times such as death, illness. The World-view of a culture performs an integrating function of providing an over-all design of living for the people. It is also adaptational in the sense that it helps to resolve conflicts and reduce internal structural contradictions that occur in the process of cultural change.[49]

In these approaches, culture is a way of life of the people, provides a world-view which Marx suggests very often as the product of a dominant class and Redfield and M.N. Srinivas believe that it has two components the "great" and the "little" traditions.

(iv) Literary Critics

There are literary critics such as Matthew Arnold, T.S. Eliot, F.R. Leavis and Raymond Williams who use the concept of culture giving other meanings applied in analysis of literature.

Matthew Arnold claimed in his book *Culture and Anarchy* that culture was the pursuit and study of perfection: "Culture being a pursuit of our total perfection by means of getting to know, on all matters which most concern us, the best which has been thought and said in the world and through this knowledge, turning a stream of fresh and free thought upon our stock notions and habits."[50] This is a social idea of culture which emphasizes on tradition as well as the need for change.

T.S. Eliot believed in the individual talent being part and parcel of the great literary tradition. "By culture, I mean first of all what the anthropologists mean, the way of life of a particular people living together in one place. Their culture is visible in their arts, in their social systems, in their habits and customs, in their religion . . . culture is more than an assemblage of the arts, customs and beliefs."[51]

F.R. Leavis confined the idea of culture to arts and literature. The 'discerning appreciation of art and literature' was now equated with culture, rather than it being the pursuit of harmonious perfection by means of such appreciation. For him, culture was no longer a process, it had become identified with the objects such as the works of literature, classics, philosophy and science that provided the basis of culture. He asserted that culture had become a property of the minority, the elite: "In any period of history, it is upon a very small minority that the discerning appreciation of art and literature depends; it is only a few who are capable of unprompted, first hand judgement."[52]

Raymond Williams indicates the three main significant usages of the concept of culture: "We need to distinguish three levels of culture even in its most general definition. There is the lived culture of a particular time and place, only fully accessible to those living in that time and place. There is the recorded culture, of every kind, from art to the most everyday facts: the culture of a period. There is also as the factor, connecting lived culture and period cultures, the culture of the selective tradition."[53] He insists on the link between the social order and culture: "Culture is a signifying system through which necessarily a social order is communicated, reproduced, experienced and explored."[54] The production of culture is to be related to the social groups. Hence the social conditions and relations must be taken into account when literature is analysed. Raymond Williams brings in a Marxist perspective of literature and culture.

(v) Working Definition of Culture

The ideas of culture proposed by the anthropologists, sociologists and literary critics give us a broad spectrum of views on the concept of culture. This indicates the exhaustive nature of the concept itself. The usage of the term 'culture' in this book will be: It is a way of life of the people (Kinsberg) of the land of South India (drawing from the meaning of the word 'culture' as cultivation of the soil, specific and particular) their specific patterns of behaviour: (Ruth Benedict) its essential core consists of traditional. historically derived and selected ideas especially their attached values (Kroeber and Kluckhohn) belonging to both "great" and "little" traditions (Redfield and M.N. Srinivas) some of which are expressed through symbols and myths (Clifford Gertz).

B. The Meaning of the Term "Value"

The next term that needs to be analysed is 'value.' The word 'value' is used in many different senses with divergent implications. Hence there is the need to specify the exact meaning in which it will be used in this book.

The Unabridged Oxford Dictionary in its supplement to volume four (1986) gives the following meanings: "entertaining, worth keeping company with, worth seeing; regarded especially in relation to an individual or a group, the principles or standards of a person or society; the personal or societal judgement of what is valuable and important in life; the quality of a thing considered in respect of its power and validity for a specified purpose or effect."[55]

The American Heritage Illustrated Encyclopeadic Dictionary states the meaning of "value" to be: "Those qualities regarded by a person or group as important and desirable; a set of standards and principles."[56]

The Webster's New Collegiate Dictionary defines the word as follows: Value comes from the Latin word 'Valere' to be worth and strong, "relative worth, utility or importance, degree of excellence, something (as a principle or quality) intrinsically valuable or deniable."[57]

According to the *Encyclopaedia of Religion and Ethics*, value is "essentially a personal attitude, as a recognition of the supremacy of the category of personality, has maintained itself and proved a clue to the labyrinth of values."[58]

The Theory of Value

The term value has been defined in terms of many concepts: value as utility, pleasure, interest, an intrinsic good; value in terms of 'approval,' the approval by an individual, approval by a majority of individuals, approval by convention: "The values are originally patterns of an ethical ideal sphere, a realm of its own structures, its own laws and order." (Nicholai Hartmann)[59] Value is also viewed as a quality of objects: quality embodied or actually present in the cognitive objects (Dewey).[60]

The meaning in which this term "values" will be used in this study will be a set of principles or standards of behaviour regarded, desirable and important, held in high esteem by South Indian society and the failure to hold them will result in blame, criticism or condemnation.

C. Assumptions

The Unabridged Oxford English Dictionary gives twelve meanings for this term. The tenth and the eleventh meanings are taken to be applicable to this analysis: "Taking anything for granted as the basis of argument or action, that which is assumed or taken for granted, a supposition, postulate."[61] "The supposition that something is true, a fact or statement (as a proposition, axiom, postulate or notion) taken for granted."[62]

The term assumptions (relevant to cultural values) in the book will mean the suppositions that are accepted to be true and taken for granted by South Indian society.

D. South Indian Novelists

South India refers to the geographical territories of Karnataka, Andhra, Kerala and Tamilnadu—the culture it represents. The novelists chosen for analysing in this book are those who were born, grew up and lived for a considerable time in one of the above states. The novels chosen for scrutiny are novels originally written in English. Translations of novels from the regional language have been completely excluded. The chart on the following page[63] gives a detailed picture of the selected South Indian novelists and their works chosen for analysis.

The reasons for the selection of these novelists are the following:

(1) These novelists are products of both cultures: the culture of their native state as well as the culture of the British which the English language brings with it.

(2) The authors can be divided into two distinctive groups: The novelists who have spent most of their lives in Tamilnadu and Karnataka, their native states with little or no exposure to the Western world. The novelists who were born in one of the states, Tamilnadu or Karnataka or Andhra, but spent most of their lives abroad, having been exposed to western thinking and values. They felt obliged to cater to the western audience. The novelists of both these groups belong to the Brahmin families which certainly conditions their perceptions. There is also a difference in perceptions of the cultural values and assumptions of South India between the novelists who have spent most of their lives in South India and those who have been away from South India.

	Sand Dunes (1923)		1930s and maintained a regular correspondence with him. Loved his wife very much	Raja Rao) interested in Russian classics especially Tolstoy and Western philosophy, studied Marxism. Married twice: Camille Mouly in 1931 and Katherine Jones in 1965		extensively in Asia. Mother by birth from Kashmir. Father by birth from Karnataka. Married the American writer Fabian Bowers in 1952. Met Sarojini Naidu as a sixteen year old girl. Imbibed the culture of the different people of Asia	
Years in India	All his lfe	All his life	Spent his life in South India till 1957. In 1960, for the first time visited Calcutta and Delhi to receive the Sahitya Akademi Award for the novel *The Guide*	First 19 years of his early life. Years of Second World War (1938-1942) and independence of India	The early years of her childhood and adolescence until she married Mr. Taylor	Early part of her life in 1939 returned to India	The early part of his life

				University of Montepellier, France, 1929-30. The Sorbonne University, 1930-33			
Employment		Served as Government official. Tried to serve in the police force twice but failed in both attempts	Teacher of English, worked in a school only for five days. Started writing for magazines and newspapers	Since 1965, Professor of Philosophy, teaching one semester a year at University of Texas, Austin	Journalist for sometime. Full-time writing under her maiden name Kamala Markandaya (Kamala Puranaiya Taylor)	Writer	Served as a member of the Indian Foreign Service in United Nations, Vienna Teaching in different Universities in U.S.A. since 1948
Special Influ-ences	Developed a negative attitude of the West and the European way of life. Very much taken up with the ideals of Gandhi, Patriotism, love for rural life and its customs; revealed in his earlier works *Paper Boats* (1921) and *Sand Dunes* (1923)	Influenced by Gandhism and love for rural life, involved in the Iyengar-Ayyar feud; Vadakalai & Tenkalai schools	Lived with his grandmother as a child in Madras Father, a Headmaster of a school captivated by the Myths and Puranas of India, the *Ramayana* and the *Mahabharata*; Friendship with the novelist Graham Greene right from the	Attracted to the religious and philosophical elements of Hinduism. Studied the French classics. Special attachment to Romain Rolland, Paul Valeri, Charles Baudelaire and Andre Malraux (a personal friend of	Father worked in the Railway—had a chance to travel to various places in India and also a good part of England and the continent. Married an Englishman, Taylor.	Father being a diplomat travelled a lot with him. He represented India in London, South Africa, Japan and U.S.A. Acted as the host-ess of her father in Tokyo. Benegal Rama Rau was the first ambassador to Japan. Travelled	Influenced greatly by Milton, T.S. Eliot and Yeats, wrote critical works on them. In 1948, joined the Indian Foreign Service and occupied various positions on behalf of the Indian Government.

	Sand Dunes (1923)		1930s and maintained a regular correspondence with him. Loved his wife very much	Raja Rao) interested in Russian classics especially Tolstoy and Western philosophy, studied Marxism. Married twice: Camille Mouly in 1931 and Katherine Jones in 1965		extensively in Asia. Mother by birth from Kashmir. Father by birth from Karnataka. Married the American writer Fabian Bowers in 1952. Met Sarojini Naidu as a sixteen year old girl. Imbibed the culture of the different people of Asia	
Years in India	All his lfe	All his life	Spent his life in South India till 1957. In 1960, for the first time visited Calcutta and Delhi to receive the Sahitya Akademi Award for the novel *The Guide*	First 19 years of his early life. Years of Second World War (1938-1942) and independence of India	The early years of her childhood and adolescence until she married Mr. Taylor	Early part of her life in 1939 returned to India	The early part of his life

				University of Montepellier, France, 1929-30. The Sorbonne University, 1930-33			
Employment		Served as Government official. Tried to serve in the police force twice but failed in both attempts	Teacher of English, worked in a school only for five days. Started writing for magazines and newspapers	Since 1965, Professor of Philosophy, teaching one semester a year at University of Texas, Austin	Journalist for sometime. Full-time writing under her maiden name Kamala Markandaya (Kamala Puranaiya Taylor)	Writer	Served as a member of the Indian Foreign Service in United Nations, Vienna Teaching in different Universities in U.S.A. since 1948
Special Influences	Developed a negative attitude of the West and the European way of life. Very much taken up with the ideals of Gandhi, Patriotism, love for rural life and its customs; revealed in his earlier works *Paper Boats* (1921) and *Sand Dunes* (1923)	Influenced by Gandhism and love for rural life, involved in the Iyengar-Ayyar feud; Vadakalai & Tenkalai schools	Lived with his grandmother as a child in Madras Father, a Headmaster of a school captivated by the Myths and Puranas of India, the *Ramayana* and the *Mahabharata*, Friendship with the novelist Graham Greene right from the	Attracted to the religious and philosophical elements of Hinduism. Studied the French classics. Special attachment to Romain Rolland, Paul Valeri, Charles Baudelaire and Andre Malraux (a personal friend of	Father worked in the Railway—had a chance to travel to various places in India and also a good part of England and the continent. Married an Englishman, Taylor.	Father being a diplomat travelled a lot with him. He represented India in London, South Africa, Japan and U.S.A. Acted as the hostess of her father in Tokyo. Benegal Rama Rau was the first ambassador to Japan. Travelled	Influenced greatly by Milton, T.S. Eliot and Yeats, wrote critical works on them. In 1948, joined the Indian Foreign Service and occupied various positions on behalf of the Indian Government.

II, p. 1247.

8. *Ibid.*, p. 1248.
9. James Hastings, ed., *Encylopaedia of Religion and Ethics* (New York: Charles Scribner's, 1951), Vol. III, p. 358.
10. Edward B. Tylor, *Primitive Culture* (London: John Murray, 1903), p. 1.
11. Milton Singer, "The Concept of Culture," *International Encyclopaedia of Social Sciences*, ed. David L. Sills (U.S.A.: Macmillan and the Free Press, 1968).
12. A.L. Krober and Clyde Kluckhohn, *Culture: A Critical Review of Concepts and Definitions*, Papers of the Peabody Museum of American Archaeology and Ethnology (Cambridge, Massachusetts: Harvard University), 47, 1 (1952).
13. Leslie A. White, "Review of A.L. Krober and Clyde Kluckhohn, *Culture: A Critical Review of Concepts and Definitions*," Ethnological Essays, ed. Beth Dillingham and Robert L. Camerio (Albuquerque: University of Mexico Press, 1987), p. 163. Originally this essay was published in *American Anthropologist* (1954), pp. 461-68.
14. A.L. Krober, and Clyde Kluckhohn, *Culture: A Critical Review of Concepts and Definitions,* p. 181.
15. Milton Singer, p. 528.
16. Krober and Kluckhohn, p. 189.
17. Melville J. Herskovits, *Man and His Works: The Science of Cultural Anthropology* (New York: Alfred A. Knopf, 1964), p. 625.
18. George Peter Murdock, "Fundamental Characteristics of Culture," *Culture and Society* (Pittsburgh: University of Pittsburgh Press, 1965), pp. 80-86.
19. Bronislaw Malinowski, "Culture," *Encyclopaedia of Social Sciences,* 4, 1931, p. 621.
20. Edward Sapir, "Culture, Genuine and Spurious," *American Journal of Sociology,* 29, 1924, p. 402, "any socially inherited element in the life of man, material and spiritual is culture."
21. Ralph Linton, *The Study of Man* (New York: D. Appleton Century, 1936), p. 78. "The Social heredity is called culture . . . culture means the total social heredity of mankind."
22. A.L. Krober, *Anthropology* (New York: Harcourt, Brace and World, 1948), p. 252. This definition is quoted by A.L. Krober in his chapter on "What is Culture." Robert H. Lowe has defined culture as social tradition in his book *Primitive Society* (1920).
23. Ruth Benedict, *Race, Science and Politics* (Rev. ed., New York: The Viking Press, 1945), p. 13. "Culture is the sociological term for learned behaviour."
24. Julian H. Steward, *Area Research: Theory and Practice,* Social Science Research Council Bulletin, U.S.A., 63, 1950, p. 98. "Culture is generally understood to mean learned modes of behaviour which are socially transmitted."
25. Allison Davis, *Social Class Influences upon Learning* (Cambridge:

(3) There are also differences in the conception of the novel form itself. To the first group of novelists such as R.K. Narayan, K.R. Venkataramani and K. Nagarajan, the novel in English remains to a large extent an authentic means of self-expression and communication in which even the English language gets indigenized. To the second group of novelists such as Raja Rao, Kamala Markandaya, Santha Rama Rau, Balachandra Rajan, the novel becomes to a great extent a communication vehicle with the western audience and an expression of nostalgia and remembrance of one's own native cultural values, which one has left behind. These differences in perception will be indicated in the following parts of the book.

The cultural values and assumptions in the selected South Indian novelists such as K.R. Venkataramani, K. Nagarajan, R.K. Narayan, Raja Rao, Kamala Markandaya, Santha Rama Rau and Balachandra Rajan are wide-ranging. They try to explore the different dimensions of South Indian behaviour and traditions. We shall discuss the following:

(a) Social Expression: the role and idea of womanhood and the significance of relationship.

(b) Literary and Traditional Aspects: the role of myths and puranas and the absorption of Tamil expressions and proverbs.

(c) The Religious and Cultural Manifestations: the role of the Guru and Asceticism and the role of Bhakti and idea of religion.

NOTES

1. Guy Amirthanayagam, "Literature as Culture," *Awakened Conscience*, ed. C.D. Narasimhaiah (New Delhi: Sterling, 1978), p. 433.
2. Paul Verghese, *Problems of the Indian Creative Writer in English* (Bombay: Somaiya, 1971), p. 110.
3. Vasant Shahane, "Indo-English Literature: Its Major Concerns and its Academic Rationale," *Alien Voice: Perspectives on Commonwealth Literature*, ed. Avadhesh K. Srivastava (Lucknow: Print House, 1981), p. 11.
4. J. Ellina Kalinikova, *Indian English Literature: A Perspective* (Ghaziabad: Vimal, 1982), p. 211.
5. *Ibid.*, p. 214. The words of Meenakshi Mukherjee are quoted by Kalinikova.
6. Krishna Rayan, "Towards an Indian Critical Tradition for Indian Writing in English," *Indian Journal of English Studies*, 25 (1985), p. 3.
7. *The Oxford English Dictionary (Unabridged): A New English Dictionary on Historical Principles* (London: Oxford University Press, 1961), vol.

II, p. 1247.
8. *Ibid.*, p. 1248.
9. James Hastings, ed., *Encylopaedia of Religion and Ethics* (New York: Charles Scribner's, 1951), Vol. III, p. 358.
10. Edward B. Tylor, *Primitive Culture* (London: John Murray, 1903), p. 1.
11. Milton Singer, "The Concept of Culture," *International Encyclopaedia of Social Sciences*, ed. David L. Sills (U.S.A.: Macmillan and the Free Press, 1968).
12. A.L. Krober and Clyde Kluckhohn, *Culture: A Critical Review of Concepts and Definitions*, Papers of the Peabody Museum of American Archaeology and Ethnology (Cambridge, Massachusetts: Harvard University), 47, 1 (1952).
13. Leslie A. White, "Review of A.L. Krober and Clyde Kluckhohn, *Culture: A Critical Review of Concepts and Definitions*," Ethnological Essays, ed. Beth Dillingham and Robert L. Camerio (Albuquerque: University of Mexico Press, 1987), p. 163. Originally this essay was published in *American Anthropologist* (1954), pp. 461-68.
14. A.L. Krober, and Clyde Kluckhohn, *Culture: A Critical Review of Concepts and Definitions*, p. 181.
15. Milton Singer, p. 528.
16. Krober and Kluckhohn, p. 189.
17. Melville J. Herskovits, *Man and His Works: The Science of Cultural Anthropology* (New York: Alfred A. Knopf, 1964), p. 625.
18. George Peter Murdock, "Fundamental Characteristics of Culture," *Culture and Society* (Pittsburgh: University of Pittsburgh Press, 1965), pp. 80-86.
19. Bronislaw Malinowski, "Culture," *Encyclopaedia of Social Sciences*, 4, 1931, p. 621.
20. Edward Sapir, "Culture, Genuine and Spurious," *American Journal of Sociology*, 29, 1924, p. 402, "any socially inherited element in the life of man, material and spiritual is culture."
21. Ralph Linton, *The Study of Man* (New York: D. Appleton Century, 1936), p. 78. "The Social heredity is called culture . . . culture means the total social heredity of mankind."
22. A.L. Krober, *Anthropology* (New York: Harcourt, Brace and World, 1948), p. 252. This definition is quoted by A.L. Krober in his chapter on "What is Culture." Robert H. Lowe has defined culture as social tradition in his book *Primitive Society* (1920).
23. Ruth Benedict, *Race, Science and Politics* (Rev. ed., New York: The Viking Press, 1945), p. 13. "Culture is the sociological term for learned behaviour."
24. Julian H. Steward, *Area Research: Theory and Practice*, Social Science Research Council Bulletin, U.S.A., 63, 1950, p. 98. "Culture is generally understood to mean learned modes of behaviour which are socially transmitted."
25. Allison Davis, *Social Class Influences upon Learning* (Cambridge:

(3) There are also differences in the conception of the novel form itself. To the first group of novelists such as R.K. Narayan, K.R. Venkataramani and K. Nagarajan, the novel in English remains to a large extent an authentic means of self-expression and communication in which even the English language gets indigenized. To the second group of novelists such as Raja Rao, Kamala Markandaya, Santha Rama Rau, Balachandra Rajan, the novel becomes to a great extent a communication vehicle with the western audience and an expression of nostalgia and remembrance of one's own native cultural values, which one has left behind. These differences in perception will be indicated in the following parts of the book.

The cultural values and assumptions in the selected South Indian novelists such as K.R. Venkataramani, K. Nagarajan, R.K. Narayan, Raja Rao, Kamala Markandaya, Santha Rama Rau and Balachandra Rajan are wide-ranging. They try to explore the different dimensions of South Indian behaviour and traditions. We shall discuss the following:

(a) Social Expression: the role and idea of womanhood and the significance of relationship.

(b) Literary and Traditional Aspects: the role of myths and puranas and the absorption of Tamil expressions and proverbs.

(c) The Religious and Cultural Manifestations: the role of the Guru and Asceticism and the role of Bhakti and idea of religion.

NOTES

1. Guy Amirthanayagam, "Literature as Culture," *Awakened Conscience*, ed. C.D. Narasimhaiah (New Delhi: Sterling, 1978), p. 433.
2. Paul Verghese, *Problems of the Indian Creative Writer in English* (Bombay: Somaiya, 1971), p. 110.
3. Vasant Shahane, "Indo-English Literature: Its Major Concerns and its Academic Rationale," *Alien Voice: Perspectives on Commonwealth Literature*, ed. Avadhesh K. Srivastava (Lucknow: Print House, 1981), p. 11.
4. J. Ellina Kalinikova, *Indian English Literature: A Perspective* (Ghaziabad: Vimal, 1982), p. 211.
5. *Ibid*., p. 214. The words of Meenakshi Mukherjee are quoted by Kalinikova.
6. Krishna Rayan, "Towards an Indian Critical Tradition for Indian Writing in English," *Indian Journal of English Studies*, 25 (1985), p. 3.
7. *The Oxford English Dictionary (Unabridged): A New English Dictionary on Historical Principles* (London: Oxford University Press, 1961), vol.

Part IV

Part IV

3. R.K. Narayan	4. *Swami and His Friends* (1935)	Grandmother of Swami	The mother of Swami				
,,	5. *The Bachelor of Arts* (1938)		The mother of Chandran				Malathi, the daughter of Krishna Iyer, the first love of Chandran
,,	6. *The Dark Room* (1938)		a) Savitri, the wife of Ramani b) Gangu c) Janamma d) Ponni, the wife of Mari	Shanta Bai		Savitri, the wife of Ramani	
,,	7. *The English Teacher* (1945)		a) Sushila, the wife of Krishnan b) The mother of Krishnan c)The mother of Sushila				The wife of the schoolmaster
,,	8. *Mr. Sampath* (1949)		a) The wife of Sampath b)The wife of Srinivas c)The mother of Rani	Shanthi, an actress			

The Spectrum of the Roles of Women

Author	Novels Chosen for Analysis	Older Women and Widows	Housewives and Mothers	The Disturbers	The Idealists	Protesters	Miscellaneous
1. K.R. Venkataramani	1. *Kandan the Patriot* (1934)	a) Porgudi, the mother of Chockan b) Neelakshi, the mother of Raghu	a) Saraswathi, the wife of Sundaram b) The wife of Raghu Kamakshi, Karian's wife		a) Rajeswari, the lover of Rangan b) Saraswathi, the wife of Sundaram		
,,	2. *Murugan, the Tiller* (1972)	Meenakshi, the mother of Janaki	a) Ponni, the wife of Murugan b)Janaki, the wife of Ramu c) Kokilam, the wife of Kedari d) Sita, the wife of vagabond husband			Kokilam, the wife of Kedari	
2. K. Nagarajan	3. *The Chronicles of Kedaram* (1961)		a) Vembu Ammal, the wife of Vanchinatha Sastri b) Mangalam, the wife of Mr. Dikshit c) Komavalli Ammal, the wife of Chari d) Alamelu, the wife of the narrator Konan e) The wife of Vasu	a) Dasi Swornam (Devadasi) b) Kamalam, the duaghter of Swornam (Devadasi)		a) Nirmala the daughter of Chari, married to an incompatible husband b) Elatha	

3. R.K. Narayan	4. *Swami and His Friends* (1935)	Grandmother of Swami	The mother of Swami				
,,	5. *The Bachelor of Arts* (1938)		The mother of Chandran				Malathi, the daughter of Krishna Iyer, the first love of Chandran
,,	6. *The Dark Room* (1938)		a) Savitri, the wife of Ramani b) Gangu c) Janamma d) Ponni, the wife of Mari	Shanta Bai		Savitri, the wife of Ramani	
,,	7. *The English Teacher* (1945)		a) Sushila, the wife of Krishnan b) The mother of Krishnan c)The mother of Sushila				The wife of the schoolmaster
,,	8. *Mr. Sampath* (1949)		a) The wife of Sampath b)The wife of Srinivas c)The mother of Rani	Shanthi, an actress			

The Spectrum of the Roles of Women

Author	Novels Chosen for Analysis	Older Women and Widows	Housewives and Mothers	The Disturbers	The Idealists	Protesters	Miscellaneous
1. K.R. Venkataramani	1. *Kandan the Patriot* (1934)	a) Porgudi, the mother of Chockan b) Neelakshi, the mother of Raghu	a) Saraswathi, the wife of Sundaram b) The wife of Raghu Kamakshi, Karian's wife		a) Rajeswari, the lover of Rangan b) Saraswathi, the wife of Sundaram		
,,	2. *Murugan, the Tiller* (1972)	Meenakshi, the mother of Janaki	a) Ponni, the wife of Murugan b)Janaki, the wife of Ramu c) Kokilam, the wife of Kedari d) Sita, the wife of vagabond husband			Kokilam, the wife of Kedari	
2. K. Nagarajan	3. *The Chronicles of Kedaram* (1961)		a) Vembu Ammal, the wife of Vanchinatha Sastri b) Mangalam, the wife of Mr. Dikshit c) Komavalli Ammal, the wife of Chari d) Alamelu, the wife of the narrator Konan e) The wife of Vasu	a) Dasi Swornam (Devadasi) b) Kamalam, the duaghter of Swornam (Devadasi)		a) Nirmala the daughter of Chari, married to an incompatible husband b) Elatha	

,,	16. *Some Inner Fury* (1956)		a) Premala, the wife of Kit b) The mother of Kit			a) Meera, the sister of Kit b) Roshan	
,,	17. A *Silence of Desire* (1960)		Sarojini, the wife of Dandekar				
,,	18. *Possession* (1963)		The mother of Valmiki				a) Lady Caroline Bell, the English woman b) Anasuya, the narrator
,,	19. *A Handful of Rice* (1966)		a) The mother-in-law of Ravi b) Nalini, the wife of Ravi c) Thangan, the sister of Nalini				
,,	20. *The Coffer Dams* (1969)						Helen, the wife of Clinton, an English woman
,,	21. *The Nowhere Man* (1972)		Vasantha, the wife of Srinivas				Mrs. Pickering, the Englishwoman
,,	22. *Two Virgins* (1973)	Aunt Alamelu	a) Mother of Saroja and Lalitha b) The wife of Manickan				a) Saroja and Lalitha b) Young women growing up

5. Balachandra Rajan	23. *The Dark Dancer* (1958)		a) Kamala, the wife of Krishnan b) The mother of Krishnan	Cynthia, an Englishwoman		Kamala	
”	24. *Too Long in the West* (1962)		Nalini, the wife of Raman, the barber				
6. Raja Rao	25. *Kanthapura* (1938)	Narasamma, the mother of Moorthy			Ratna, Rangamma, the women of Kanthapura		
”	26. *The Serpent and the Rope* (1963)	The Little Mother				Saroja Sukumari	a) Savitri b) Madeline, the French woman c) The wife of Ramaswamy
”	27. *The Cat and Shakespeare* (1965)		a) The wife of Ramakrishna Pai b) The wife of Govindan Nair				Santha, the mistress of Ramakrishna Pai
”	28. *Comrade Kirillov* (1976)		Irene, the wife of Kirillov				

4.3. The Spectrum of the Roles of Women

If we take these roles, each role appears to manifest certain cultural values and assumptions. The older women and widows are generally affectionate, devoted, religious, set in their ways of thinking and behaviour. The housewives and mothers are submissive, docile and obedient, focused on their husbands and families, managing their households and having their own norms for private and public behaviour. The disturbers are women who disturb social peace and harmony, luring men into sexual relationships, often belonging to the class of devadasis (the dancing girls). The idealists are women who come out of the societal restrictions and dedicate their lives to great causes. The protesters are women who are rebellious and want to liberate themselves from the male-dominated society. They make their independent choices and decisions. Some of them fight for liberation but finally give up and reconcile themselves to the status quo. Some others assert their own individualities. The summary of the chart reveals the predominant stereotype that occurs in most of the novels is the housewife and the mother. This is also an indication of the affirmation of the archetypal image of the mother.

Number of Novels	28
Novelists	6
Older Women and Widows	10
Housewives and Mothers	46
Disturbers	7
Protesters	10
Idealists	6
Miscellaneous	11

Some of the characters fall into different categories at the same time. The idea and role of women cannot be restricted to the housewife and the mother as it is evident from the chart. Hence the questions that arise for our discussion are what are the cultural values and assumptions that the predominant stereotype exemplifies? To what extent are women submissive and obedient? To what extent do the novelists emphasize or challenge this dimension and role of womanhood? If they challenge this stereotype, what are the variations they present in the novels. we will attempt to answer these questions in the following discussion.

4.4. The Housewife and the Mother: Husband and Family Focused

The role of a woman as wife and mother is directed toward attachment to family, submissiveness to husband, devotion to children and in the efficient management of the household. Sushila in *The English Teacher* (R.K. Narayan) tries to run a household on a narrow budget, makes plans about their future, dreams about a house to be built and her daughter, Leela's marriage. Even after her death, she tries to communicate with her husband through a medium as a spirit. "The Lady wants to say that she is deeply devoted to her husband and child and the family as ever. She watches over them and prays for their welfare."[3] Vembu Ammal, the wife of Vanchinatha Sastri, in *The Chronicles of Kedaram* (K. Nagarajan) submits to everything in her husband including his extra marital relationship with Dasi Swornam, a public woman.[4] Sarojini, the wife of Dandekar in *A Silence of Desire* (Kamala Markandaya) is a devoted wife and dutiful mother of three children. "She was a good wife, Sarojini. Good with children, an excellent cook, an efficient manager of his household, a woman who still gave him pleasure after fifteen years of marriage, less from the warmth of her response than from her unfailing acquiescence to his demands. . . . Sarojini came to him when he wanted her placidly."[5]

Janaki, the wife of Ramu is a husband-focused woman in *Murugan the Tiller* (K.R. Venkataramani). She refers to the mythical parallel of Rama and Sita in *The Ramayana* to describe her devotion to the husband.[6] Premala the wife of Kit in *Some Inner Fury* (Kamala Markandaya) makes a constant effort to please her husband in all his anglicized ways of visiting the club's formal dinners and playing tennis.[7] She submits herself to the elaborate wedding ceremony. She is deeply religious and prays when she receives the *thali* from her husband. (50)

The tying of the *thali* is an important and essential ceremony in the wedding ritual in South India. The virgin becomes a married woman (Cumankali) benevolent and most auspicious. The word cumankali means "She who is auspicious. This auspiciousness is predicted on two factors: possession of a husband and of children . . . the state of cumankali depends not on woman's own being as female, but on women in relation to other, particularly husband and children."[8] Premala believes in the sanctity of marriage and tramples her identity in her heroic effort to please her husband. Vasantha the wife of Srinivas in *The Nowhere Man* (Kamala Markandaya) is forced to live with her husband in England. She clings tenaciously to her culture by carrying the code of conduct of a humble and submissive wife to please her husband at all times and at all costs.[9] Kamala Markandaya's portrayal of Vasantha and Premala reminds us of the nostalgic memories of the author herself of South India, its values and customs as she is living for a long time in England.

Margayya's wife in *The Financial Expert* (R.K. Narayan) believes in letting things happen and accepts them with resignation. She allows her husband to become greedy which ends in his ruin.[10] She watches passively the growing conflict between her husband, Margayya and her son Balu. (113)

The stereotype of a housewife and mother is illustrated in Rukmani representing the rural poor (Kamala Markandaya, *Nectar in a Sieve*) and Nalini representing the urban poor (Kamala Markandaya, *A Handful of Rice*). Rukmani, the wife of Nathan, a tenant farmer encounters drought, famine, torrential rains, the loss of her sons and the barrenness of her daughter, Ira. She watches her daughter, Ira, becoming a prostitute driven by hunger and destitution. She endures the infidelity of her husband. She leaves the village in search of livelihood to the town, ending in the death of her husband. She goes through all these sufferings and trials, passively and perseveringly as a loyal wife and dutiful mother.[11] Nalini the wife of Ravi, is a victim of poverty and ill-treatment of her husband. Her life is a living death. She accepts everything passively.[12]

Women are presented as passive beings struggling against the odds of life silently. Kamala Markandaya seems to be preoccupied with the social forces at work, the unjust social system, rural poverty and famine, the impact of urbanization and industrialization on the rural scene. Her portrayal lacks the intimacy and the earthiness of the presentation of the novelists like R.K. Narayan, K.R. Venkataramani because of her years abroad. "Her accounts of the poor peasant woman as well as the slum-dweller have been found fault with as having patches of narration which do not ring true. She has also been accused of tailoring her material to fit a western public. Her constant negative account of Indian life and her seemingly facile equation of evil with economic backwardness . . . have also been disputed."[13]

The loving and caring figure of the mother is illustrated in Raju's Mother (R.K. Narayan, *The Guide*) and the Little Mother (Raja Rao, *The Serpent and the Rope*). Raju remembers her kindness and love for him even after a long time.[14] The Little Mother loves all the children of the joint-family. Ramaswamy, the eldest son is devoted to his stepmother. "My new stepmother loved me very dearly and I could not think of a home without her bright smile."[15] Since motherhood is exalted and venerated, the barren woman is considered a curse. She is potentially malevolent and inauspicious, while living and after death may impede the fertility of all spheres.[16] Barrenness brings discredit to a woman. This could be seen in the case of Ambika (R.K. Narayan, *The Vendor of Sweets*) who gets a son after a long time after her vows to the God on Badri Hill.[17] Ira, the daughter of Rukmani (Kamala Markandaya, *Nectar in a Sieve* is sent back to her mother by her husband because of barrenness. (126)

When we look at the predominant stereotype of a housewife and mother in the novels, womanhood emerges to be a relational concept. No woman exists independently of a man or a man's influence. Women are always considered in relation to their husbands and children in South Indian society. Hence, dependency on husbands and children becomes a cultural value in the predominant stereotype of a housewife and mother.

4.5. Variations of the Predominant Stereotype

The novelists challenge this stereotype in different ways. The submissiveness and the unquestioning obedience, passivity of a woman is seriously questioned when they present women in their private and public behaviour, as protesters and idealists and under the influence of western and urban values.

Women who are humble and obedient housewives and dutiful mothers have their own code of conduct and behaviour in private with their husbands. Very often they have their ways. Sushila, the wife of Krishnan (R.K. Narayan, *The English Teacher*) has her way with her husband in the following incident. She sells an old timepiece for twelve annas. It is considered by Krishnan as a relic. Krishnan gets upset and reacts to her. "What is the use of crying, after committing a serious blunder." (52) She immediately retorts: "What do you care, what use it is or not. If I had known, you cared more for a dilapidated clock." (53) It is only Krishnan who takes the initiative for peace. Sarojini, the wife of Dandekar (Kamala Markandaya, *A Silence of Desire*) keeps a public profile of a passive wife and devoted mother. In private life, she asserts her individuality and makes her husband conform to her way of thinking and behaviour. When she has a sudden inexplicable growth in her womb, she goes to a Swami, a faith healer. She keeps the visits a well-guarded secret. Though her husband disapproves of her visits and suspects her of infidelity, she keeps on going to the Swami regularly. She goes for a surgical operation not because Dandekar wants it but because of the assurance of Swami that everything will go well. She confronts directly the rationalistic way of thinking of her husband by her private behaviour. She tells her husband: "I do not expect you to understand—you with your Western notions, your superior talk of ignorance and superstition when it all means that you don't know what lies beyond reason and you prefer not to find out." (87)

Ambika, the wife of Jagan and the mother of Mali (R.K. Narayan,

The Vendor of Sweets) is a dutiful wife and a faithful daughter-in-law. She exercises control over her husband in private. When Jagan recollects the happy married life with her at the end of the novel, makes a comment on her private behaviour. "After all these years of married life, he could not anticipate her reactions. Sometimes she took things easily with the greatest cheer; sometimes she stung him and glared at him for the same remark. She was a model of goodness, courtesy and cheerfulness generally, but she could lash with her tongue when her temper was roused." (166)

The private behaviour of a housewife and mother is at variance with her public image and conventional behaviour, as it is shown in the above discussion.

Thus the private behaviour of having their own way with their husbands is a distinctive cultural trait of the South Indian women. The novelists go beyond the predominant stereotype of a housewife and mother. The submissiveness and docility of the women come into question. The novelists also present women in different light as idealists embodying in themselves the values of sacrifice and dedication to a great cause. This presentation differs from the predominant stereotype. These women appear in the novels in the context of the freedom movement. The impact of Gandhi in their lives makes them transcend their social barriers and taboos and dedicate themselves to the great cause of the freedom of India. Rajeswari and Saraswathi (K.R. Venkataramani, *Kandan, the Patriot*) are women of great idealism. Rajeswari, a well educated girl, is ready to turn down the offer of Rangan for marriage who is madly in love with her. She tells Kandan: "The love of the mother, Kanda, the grand passion for my country fills my being and floods my heart night and day, like the sea that ebbs and flows into the little creek at the mouth of the river. I must work for the freedom of my country first, for which I must have my own freedom."[18] Rajeswari also inspires Rangan to follow her in struggling for the freedom of the Motherland. Sarawathi is prepared to stake everything to join the freedom struggle, "a first class patriot, a seer, a magnet force and an organizing genius of the first order." (202) Bharati (R.K. Narayan, *Waiting for the Mahatma*) emerges during the days of independence struggle. She comes under the spell of Mahatma Gandhi. Sriram falls in love with her at first sight. While she is touched by his romantic nature, she wages a ceaseless battle to uplift his mind. She inspires him, teaches him to spin, to be self sufficient and to adapt to the Gandhian way of living.[19] She waits for the permission of the Mahatma and the blessing for their marriage and makes him also wait.

Raja Rao in his *Kanthapura* makes the village women under the leadership of Rangamma break out openly to support the freedom struggle led by Moorthy. The men are surprised at this move. Rangamma inspires the other women. "We think of nothing but the blowpipe and the broomstick and the milking of the many cows. We too should organize a Volunteer Corps."[20] They flout the order of the government and march ahead—mothers, aunts, sisters and grandmothers and the police beat them up. The women are shown to be united in idealism and patriotism. They become a mighty and irresistible force. This is a revolutionary portrait of women during the freedom struggle by Raja Rao, in opposition to the predominant stereotype.

The Protesters

The women who rebel against the social structure and male-dominated society are in direct contrast to the predominant stereotype. There are two groups of women in this category who seek for liberation: the women who fight for liberation but finally give up and reconcile themselves to the status quo; the women who make their own independent decisions and assert their individualities. Savitri (R.K. Narayan, *The Dark Room*), Saroja (Raja Rao, *The Serpent and the Rope*) and Kamala (Balachandra Rajan, *The Dark Dancer*) belong to the first group. Savitri is not able to tolerate the domineering, selfish and callous nature of her husband Ramani. She resists the idea of Ramani: "India owed its spiritual eminence to the fact that the people here realized that a woman's primary duty (also a divine privilege) was being a mother and a wife and what woman retained the right of being called a wife who disobeyed her husband? Didn't all the ancient epics and scriptures enjoin upon the woman, the strictest identification with her husband? He remembered all the heroines of the epics whose one dominant quality was a blind stubborn following of their husbands, like the shadow following the substance."[21] She is all the time struggling against the oppression. (73) She reacts violently to him when she discovers his relationship with Shanta Bai, a woman at the office: "I'm a human being. You men will never grant that. For you, we are playthings when you feel like hugging and slaves at other times. Don't think you can fondle us when you like and kick us when you choose."

She leaves home, attempts to commit suicide and is rescued. Finally, she comes back home. "She pockets her pride and returns home thoroughly deflated and humiliated, prepared to accept the status quo, to accept life with Ramani and Shanta Bai. Her rebellion is all too brief."[22] In the portrayal of Savitri, R.K. Narayan shows himself to be a novelist who knows intimately the Tamil household. He is able to capture the desire for liberation and the inability to liberate themselves in the character of Savitri. Being a writer who has stayed for long immersed in his native culture, he is able to give a realistic presentation of the struggling women. (77) The novelist demonstrates "the cyclical view of life . . . why rebel if nothing changes, if underneath the old norms persist even though they prove to be restrictive and inhibiting."[23] Saroja, the sister of Ramaswamy complies with an arranged marriage. She does not like her betrothed but finally goes through the wedding ceremonies and reconciles herself and tells her brother: "I shall bring but a fair name to the household." (269) She is ready to forego all her likes and dislikes for the sake of the honor of the family. Raja Rao, having spent most of his life in the West, tries to voice forth the western idea of liberation of women being independent of the family and the society but finally reconciles himself to the South Indian situation. Kamala, the wife of Krishnan accepts the suffering inflicted on her by her husband's faithfulness. She proves the words of the Tamil proverb "A husband commands respect at all times even if the husband happens to be a piece of stone or a blade of grass."[24] She silently protests and goes to the Hindu-Muslim conflict ridden area to serve the victims. When Krishnan comes back, she reconciles to the situation. "There was no bitterness, no resentment, not even curiosity about the manner of her defeat."[25] Balachandra Rajan looks at Kamala nostalgically, having lived so many years outside India, without being able to enter into the inner struggle of Kamala as R.K. Narayan does with Savitri.

The second category of women become very independent in their decisions and fight for their liberation. Ira (Kamala Markandaya, *Nectar in a Sieve*), Daisy (R.K. Narayan, *The Painter of Signs*), Nalini (Balachandra Rajan, *Too Long in the West*) and Mira (Kamala Markandaya, *Some Inner Fury*), are some of the illustrations of the women who assert their individualities. Ira becomes a prostitute when she finds her family in hunger and destitution. She makes her own independent choice. She does not consult or wait for the approval of her parents Nathan and Rukmani. "To-night and tomorrow and every night, so long as there is need. I will not hunger any more." (103) These are her decisive words when she is confronted by her father Nathan who calls her a harlot and a common strumpet. Daisy asserts her independence by choosing her career as an ardent propagator of population control. She puzzles Raman, her lover. "She is a rare type of girl, devoted to the service of people and that is all her religion. . . . Her worship takes the form of service to the poor and the ignorant and helping them live a decent life."[26] She declares her purpose to Raman. "Long ago, I broke away from the routine of a woman's life. There are millions of women who go through it happily. I am not one of them. I have planned for myself a different kind of life." (159) "I would like to work, rather than be a wife." (130) Nalini, a girl from Columbia comes back to Mudalur, an obscure little village. She subjects herself to a parody of Swayamvara. She chooses Raman, a barber, ear-piercer-cum-half-baked local revolutionary. She tries to rule her mad husband and her equally muddled village. This is a picture of fantasy presented by Balachandra Rajan, a novelist who has spent long years abroad. The portrayal is a caricature and far-fetched. Though Nalini makes an independent choice of her husband, the choice does not indicate a liberated woman. Mira falls in love with an Englishman, Richard. She does not forget the place the woman is given in the traditional South Indian family in spite of her exposure to western ideas. At the height of the struggle for independence, she is able to renounce her love for Richard for the sake of her country. "You belong to one side if you don't belong to the other. . . . There is no in between."[27] The idea of liberation is demonstrated through the independent choices these women make. The struggle against the social-structure and male-dominated society are very much the idea of liberation that comes from the west. The western idea of liberation is economic liberation. The South Indian idea of liberated womanhood is illustrated in the person of Kannaki in the epic *Cilappatikaram*. "It is Kannaki, the woman, the human heroine, who alone matters to the poet, it is Kannaki who backed by the sympathy of the entire people at Madurai, performs her duty and avenges the death of her husband. . . . She finally conquers and overthrows the law of Karma, she who enforces Gods and fate to capitulate."[28] The concept of liberation expounded in the model of Kannaki is an act of devotion to her husband. She is able to act at the height of her conviction against all odds. The burning of Madurai is a spiritual affirmation of her behaviour that is cosmic which supports and justifies her action. The liberation achieved is moral and spiritual. The women presented by the novelists, attempting at liberation in contrast to the predominant stereotype of a housewife and mother do not convey the above idea of liberation. The concept of liberation presented by them is very much influenced by the western idea of autonomy and economic independence to women away from the family and the society.

The Influence of Urban Values

Saroja and Lalitha, the two sisters (Kamala Markandaya, *Two Virgins*) grow into womanhood influenced by the values of the city. The story of the novel traces the sexual education and initiation of Saroja and Lalitha. Saroja's natural curiosity about her world includes questions about her own body, about the taboo subjects of child birth, birth control, and intercourse. Her sensitive eyes and ears pick up a lot of information quietly. Lalitha, her elder sister, learns in a more dramatic way. Her vanity and disposition of a sensual nature leads her to believe that the glamorous world she imagines outside the village is a far better one. She listens to the suggestion of her fashionable teacher, Miss Mendonza. She becomes an easy prey to the false promises of the film maker, Mr. Gupta. She follows her illusions and runs away to the city to become a film star. She returns to the village broken, bereft of both her psychic and physical innocence, even to the point of aborting her child. The novelist contrasts the innocence of the village with the sophistication and glamorous appearances of the city: ever present hunger for novelty and experimentation. "The authentic life in the village, even with its provisional ignorance, triumphs over the life-destroying or corrupting values symbolized by the city."[29] The novel reflects the process of Kamala Markandaya's liberation as a woman—her emancipation as a woman accompanied by her journalistic and political activities during the struggle for independence. She believes that emancipation comes slowly to the villages.[30] This is certainly a western perspective of understanding rural women. Unlike R.K. Narayan, one could feel the distance and aloofness of Kamala Markandaya in presenting the idea of womanhood and liberation in South India. Sexual emancipation is certainly a western idea which Kamala Markandaya brings to this novel.

Women are also presented as older women steeped in tradition, widows who do not have a status in society, disturbers of domestic harmony, gossiping, quarrelsome and ambitious women. The older women exemplify the values of affection, attachment to tradition, zeal for the honour and fair name of the family. The aunt of Raman (R.K. Narayan, *The Painter of Signs*) is very much attached to Raman and devoted to him. (165) Being a woman steeped in tradition, she cannot accept Raman loving Daisy, a girl who belongs to a different caste. She decides to leave the house because she could not think for a moment to live under the same roof with Daisy. The Grandmother of Swami (R.K. Narayan, *Swami and Friends*) is fond of Swami, her grandson, and interested in telling him all about her past and stories from the puranas.[31] The grandmother of Sriram (R.K. Narayan, *Waiting for the Mahatma*) feels intensely the separation of her grandson when he joins the independence movement for the sake of Bharati whom he loves. Raju's mother (R.K. Narayan, *The Guide*) is steeped in tradition. When Rosie leaves her husband, Marco, and comes to the home of Raju, she advises her about the importance of rejoining her husband, Marco. "She began to allude to the problems of husband and wife whenever she spoke to Rosie and filled the time with anecdotes about husbands . . . but it was always the wife, by her doggedness, perseverance and patience, that brought him around. She quoted numerous mythological stories of Savitri, Sita and all the well-known heroines." (137) She leaves home when she learns the affair between Raju and Rosie whom she considers as a tainted woman. She is so hateful of Rosie and the criticism of the neighbours because of her zeal for the honour of the family. (152)

R.K. Narayan gives a convincing portrayal of older women because of his personal and intimate experience with his own grandmother. "She had an absolute passion to teach and mould a young mind."[32] The portrayal of the older women in his novels is a compendium of all the qualities that he observed and experienced in his own grandmother.

The Widow is considered to be inauspicious in the South Indian cultural context. "The widow is the most inauspicious of all beings."[33] "The very word 'widow' (*Vitavai*): capricious power: the most inauspicious of all inauspicious things."[34] A Tamil proverb says that a widow lives only to be a cook of another widower.[35] Aunt Alamelu (Kamala Markandaya, *Two Virgins*) and the Little Mother (Raja Rao, *The Serpent and the Rope*) are convincing portrayals of the negative value of widowhood and the lack of status in society. Aunt Alamelu lives under the protection of her sister and brother-in-law. She feels not wanted and accepted. "I am only a widower, less than the dust, so do not torment yourself about my fate, Brother and she pulled her sari over her head like the poor widow that she was."[36] She has no freedom to express her opinions in the house. She has no status at home. (13) The Little Mother, being a widow is unable to participate fully in the wedding of her step-daughter, Saroja. She keeps herself in the hiding. The guests go in search of her.[37]

Women are also shown to be disturbers possessing a great capacity to allure men into sexual relationships and affect the domestic harmony. Shanta Bai (R.K. Narayan, *The Dark Room*) is portrayed as a temptress to take away Ramani, the husband of Savitri. She seizes every opportunity to manipulate Ramani. Shanta Bai reminds one of Madhavi who takes away Kovalan from his wife, Kannaki, in the Tamil classic, *Cilappatikaram*. Shantha, the actress floors Sampath, the film maker. He is so much taken up with her that he tells his friend that he will have two establishments: "Well I am going to have different establishments that I am doing nothing illegal, to feel apologetic."[38]

There is a special category of women presented by the novelists, the 'Devadasis': the temple dancers. R.K. Narayan points out in the story of Rosie *(The Guide)*, the devadasi woman, has two distinct attitudes to her person and life. Rosie is aware of the shame and the indignity of being a devadasi. She tells Raju: "I belong to a family traditionally dedicated to the temples as dancers; my mother, grandmother and before her, her mother. Even as a young girl, I danced in our village temple . . . we are considered as public women . . . we are not considered respectable; we are not considered civilized." (75) She is considered to be a temptress "the snake woman" and a disturber of domestic harmony by Raju's mother and her uncle who represent the traditional South Indian family. (150) The attitude of Rosie herself to her person and life is one of struggle to conform herself to the demands of a domestic life as a housewife (106) and the need to assert herself as an individual through her art as a professional dancer. She tries hard to prove it through her art as a professional dancer. She tries hard to prove that through education and professionalism, one can overcome the stigma of being a devadasi.

Dasi Swornam (K. Nagarajan, *The Chronicles of Kedaram*) the mistress of Vanchinatha Sastri is a well-known woman in Kedaram. The devadasis come together to present themselves to Gandhi who comes to Kedaram. (180) Rangi, the dancing girl (R.K. Narayan, *The Man-Eater of Malgudi*) accepts her way of life as a devadasi and is willing to undergo all the insults heaped on her. She is the mistress of Vasu, the taxidermist.

This whole class of women 'Devadasis' alluded to by the novelists like R.K. Narayan and K. Nagarajan, have been very much part of the South Indian village culture. They show the ambivalent attitude of the South Indian society with regard to its women, exalting them as paragons of virtue and chastity as well as exploiting them as devadasis and condemning their lives and behaviour and considering them as disturbers of domestic harmony. One could experience the contradiction in the glorification of womanhood as a housewife and mother as well as using women as objects of pleasure.

Women are also portrayed as gossiping, quarrelsome and ambitious. The ordinary village women who go to the stream or the river to bathe or to fetch drinking water, make the river front, the forum for exchange of views, opinions and gossip. K.R. Venkataramani in *Murugan, the Tiller* presents a bunch of them involved in gossiping about other women. "No wonder . . . that what others reserve for the tea-table, Hindu ladies preserve for their daily river-bath the exchange of the day's news." (55) Kamala Markandaya in *Nectar in a Sieve* depicts the companions of Rukmani, Kali, Janaki, Kunthi who come to the river to bathe and wash and indulge in gossip. (11) They indulge in talking about their husbands and inform Rukmani of the fuss that Nathan, her husband made before she came to the village. R.K. Narayan in *The Eng-*

lish Teacher portrays the wife of the schoolmaster who is domineering and cantankerous. She blames her husband for everything. (164) Janaki's mother, Meenakshi (K.R. Venkataramani, *Murugan, the Tiller*) drives her son-in-law, Ramu, to sell the land in the village and to look for a brighter career in town. Her influence is so much on Ramu, he feels her loss after her death. (138) The ambition of Janaki goads Ramu to become a camp clerk. Women given to gossip, quarrelsomeness, ambition goes beyond the predominant stereotype of a humble and submissive wife and a devoted mother.

4.6. Women: Upholders of Religious Tradition

The religious tradition is one of the strongest features of South Indian society. Religion is rated at the top in the lives of the people. It is manifested in the pujas, the religious festivals, the pilgrimages and the vows that are made by the people. The religious tradition has its vitality and power because of the significant role of women and their contribution. They consider religion as real, an ever present reality. They do not merely take refuge in religion from the woes and worries nor do they use religion to neutralize pain and sorrow. They are conscious of the ever present reality of the miracle: the intervention of god on their behalf. The following examples could be cited from the selected novels. Ambika, the wife of Jagan (R.K. Narayan, *The Vendor of Sweets*) has to wait for ten years for her off-spring. She makes a solemn vow during her visit to the god on Badri Hill. She would offer to the god, if she is given a child, an offering equivalent in weight of the child of gold, silver and corn. She fulfills her vow, when her son is born, so typical of a South Indian woman to-day. (168-69) She believes in the miracle. Rukmani (Kamala Markandaya, *Nectar in a Sieve*) has a deep sense of religion and god, even when her daughter, Ira, comes back home as a barren woman, rejected by her husband. Rukmani says: "We are all in god's hands and He is merciful." (54) Sarojini (Kamala Markandaya, *A Silence of Desire*) is a woman of faith. She tends the *tulasi* plant (the ever green plant) at the backyard of her house, respecting it as the presence of the divine. In spite of her husband, Dandekar's dislike, she did not make any difference "between the reverence due to a symbol and to its actuality, between the *tulasi* tree and its Maker." (8) The life ambition of the aunt of Raman (R.K. Narayan, *The Painter of Signs*) and the Little Mother (Raja Rao, *The Serpent and the Rope*) appears to be going to Benares on a pilgrimage. The Aunt of Raman tells him: "A visit to Kasi is the end. . . . It is the ambition of everyone of my generation to conclude this existence in Kasi, to be finally dissolved in the Ganges. That is the most auspicious end to one's life." (152) The simple possessions of the Aunt of Raman indicate her practice of religion: a couple of white saris, a little brass casket containing sacred ash for smearing on her forehead, a coral rosary for prayers, a book of sacred verse and two tiny silver images of Krishna and Ganesha. (164) The Little Mother goes with Ramaswamy, her step-son, to Benares for a pilgrimage. (6-7)

The predominant stereotype that emerges out of the novelists chosen for discussion is the housewife and the mother embodying the cultural values of being husband and family focused. This stereotype alone is not enough to explain the idea and the role of womanhood in South Indian cultural context. Hence the novelists present the following variations from the above stereotype: the private and public behaviour of women; the protest of women for liberation from the male-dominated society, women capable of great sacrifices for a worthy cause; the influence of the urban values of novelty, glamour of the city, sexual emancipation of the young village woman; the older women steeped in tradition; widows having no status in society, women who are disturbers of domestic harmony; the devadasis, women who are quarrelsome, gossiping and ambitious. Women are also portrayed as the transmitters of a deep religious tradition in South India. These contrasting images make it difficult for us to formulate a general concept of the idea and role of women in South India. However, there is enough justification to affirm the typology in all these images which is the concept of the mother that is archetypal. This concept lies behind the fertility cult latent in the collective unconscious mind of the South Indian people.

NOTES

1. Shantha Krishnaswamy, *Glimpses of Indian Women in India* (New Delhi: Asia, 1983), p. 7.
2. *Ibid.*, Abstract, p. viii
3. R.K. Narayan, *The English Teacher* (Mysore: Indian Thought Publications, 1955), p. 131.
4. K. Nagarajan. *The Chronicles of Kedaram* (Bombay: Asia), p. 198.
5. Kamala Markandaya, *A Silence of Desire* (New York: John Day, 1960), p. 10.
6. K.R. Venkataramani, *Murugan the Tiller* (London: Simpkin, Marshall, Hamilton Kent, 1927), p. 65.
7. Kamala Markandaya, *Some Inner Fury* (New York: Signet Books, 1956), p. 38.
8. Baker Holly Reynolds, "The Auspicious Married Woman," *The Powers of Tamil Women*, ed. Susan S. Wadley (Syracuse: Maxwell School of Citizenship and Public Affairs, 1980), p. 38.

9. Kamala Markandaya, *The Nowhere Man* (Bombay: Orient Longman, 1975), p. 232.
10. R.K. Narayan, *The Financial Expert* (New York: Noonday Press, 1964), p. 120.
11. Kamala Markandaya, *Nectar in a Sieve* (New York: Signet Books), p. 111.
12. Kamala Markandaya, *A Handful of Rice* (New York: The John Day Company, 1966), p. 243.
13. Shantha Krishnaswamy, *Glimpses of Women in India*, p. 167.
14. R.K. Narayan, *The Guide* (Mysore: Indian Thought Publications, 1958), p. 19.
15. Raja Rao, *The Serpent and the Rope* (New York: Pantheon Books, 1963), p. 7.
16. Baker Holly Reynolds, "The Auspicious Married Woman," p. 36.
17. R.K. Narayan, *The Vendor of Sweets* (New York: Viking Press, 1967), pp. 168-69.
18. K.R. Venkataramani, *Kandan, the Patriot* (Madras: Svetaranya Ashrama, 1934), p. 13.
19. R.K. Narayan, *Waiting for the Mahatma* (Mysore: Indian Thought Publications, 1964), p. 167.
20. Raja Rao, *Kanthapura* (London: Oxford University Press, 1963), p. 150.
21. R.K. Narayan, *The Dark Room* (New Delhi: Orient Paperbacks, 1976), p. 93.
22. Shantha Krishnaswamy, *Glimpses of Women in India*, p. 111
23. Raja Rao, *The Serpent and the Rope*, p. 255.
24. C.S. Lakshmi, *The Face behind the Mask: Women in Tamil Literature* (New Delhi: Vikas, 1984), p. 2.
25. Balachandra Rajan, *The Dark Dancer* (Greenword Press, 1970), p. 142.
26. R.K. Narayan, *The Painter of Signs* (Mysore: Indian Thought Publications, 1977), p. 153.
27. Kamala Markandaya, *Some Inner Fury*, p. 147.
28. Kamil Veith Zvelebil, *The Smile of Murugan: On Tamil Literature of South India* (Leiden: E.J. Brill, 1973), p. 174.
29. D.M. Burjorjee, "Kamala Markandaya: *Two Virgins*," *World Literature Written in English*, 13, 2 (November 1974), p. 229.
30. *Ibid.*, p. 230
31. R.K. Narayan, *Swami and Friends* (Mysore: Indian Thought Publications, 1964), p. 126.
32. R.K. Narayan, *My Days* (Mysore: Indian Thought Publications, 1975), p. 11.
33. Susan S. Wadley, "The Paradoxical Powers of Tamil Women," *The Powers of Tamil Women*, p. 154.
34. Baker Holly Reynolds, "The Auspicious Married Woman," p. 36.
35. C.S. Lakshmi, *The Face behind the Mask: Women in Tamil Literature*, p. 2.
36. Kamala Markandaya, *Two Virgins* (New Delhi: Vikas, 1983), p. 29.
37. Raja Rao, *The Serpent and the Rope*, pp. 254-55.
38. R.K. Narayan, *Mr. Sampath* (Mysore: Indian Thought Publications, 1956), p. 72.

The Significance of Relationship

5.1. The Importance of Relationship

Relationship is a core cultural value in South India. It gives a form of identity and provides security and honour. Security means the certainty that a person has that he or she will not be rejected by those related to him under any circumstances. Honour is due simply through relationship and is not affected by intelligence, money or one's contribution to the family. For most westerners, occupation is the primary form of identification. By contrast, for most South Indians, occupation is a subsidiary form of identification to relationship. To speak about a person without talking about his relationship as a husband, wife, son, or daughter would be far less frequent in the South Indian cultural context. For example, whether in school or college records, military, prison or office records, the relationship of the individual in question is invariably mentioned and he/she is recorded as son, daughter, wife of . . . etc. In the villages, families are traditionally known by their relationships: great grandfather-grandmother-father and so on. There is a persistent pre-occupation with relationship except in the case of persons who make a spiritual commitment in pursuit of the divine, abdicating their greatest source of worldly identity, i.e., relationship.

The pervasiveness of this cultural value of relationship can be seen in the novels chosen for our study. The novels tend to be stories of relationship enduring under stress and duress. The sequence of changing relationships becomes a central concern of our novelists. South Indian characters rarely exist as separate individuals as is frequently the case of the western ones. Our characters often introduce and talk about themselves and behave in terms of relationships, whether through birth or marriage. Hence it is appropriate to analyse the cultural value of relationship and its significance in the novels. The chart on the following pages reveals the intricate web of relationships.

The Aspects of Significant Relationships

Author	Title of the Novel	Central Character	Primary Characters	Secondary Characters	Caste Identity
1. K.R. Venkataramani	1. *Kandan, the Patriot* (1934)	Kandan	*Husband and wife*: Saraswathi and Sundaram Raghu and his wife *Lovers*: Rangan and Rajeswari	*Mother and sons*: Neelakshi and Raghu and Padma Porkudi and Chockan *Brother and sister*: Saraswathi and Ranga *Mother-in-law and daughter-in-law*: Neelakshi and Raghu's wife *Brother and brother*: Padma and Raghu	Untouchability (Pannial) dealt with at a great length
"	2. *Murugan, the Tiller* (1927)	*Husband and wife*: Janki and Ramu Ponnu and Murugan	*Husband and wife*: Kedari and Kokilam Sita and her husband	*Mother and daughter*: Meenakshi and Janaki *Master and servant*: Ramu and Murugan	Untouchability Padayachi and Palli
2. K. Nagarajan	3. *The Chronicles of Kedaram* (1961)	*Husband and wife*: Vanchinatha Sastri and Vembu Ammal	*Husband and wife*: Konan and Alamelu Vasu and his wife *Father and son*: Konan and his father	*Extra-marital*: Vanchinatha Sastri and Devadasi Swornam Vasu and Nirmala Chari	Caste system

3. R.K. Narayan	4. *Swami and Friends* (1935)	*Father and son*: Swami and his father *Mother and son*: Swami and his mother		*Grandmother*: Swami and his grandmother *Master and servant*: Rajam and Swami's parents	
”	5. *The Bachelor of Arts* (1937)	Mother and father of Chandran	*Lovers*: Chandran and Malathi	Elders and the young	Caste system
”	6. *The Dark Room* (1938)	*Husband and wife*: Ramani and Savitri *Parents and children*: The children of Ramani and Savitri	*Extra-Marital*: Ramani and Shanta Bai	*Husband and wife*: Gangu and her husband Janamma and her husband Ponni and Mari	Caste system Ponni and Mari
”	7. *The English Teacher* (1945)	*Husband and wife*: Sysguka and her husband, Krishnan	*Parents and children*: Sushila, Krishnan and their daughter	*Mother and son*: Krishnan and his mother *Mother-in-law and daughter-in-law*: Sushila and Krishnan's mother *Mother-in-law and son-in-law*: Krishnan and Sushila's mother	
”	8. *Mr. Sampath* (1949)		*Husband and wife*: Sampath and his wife Srinivas and his wife	*Mother and son*: Ravi and his mother *Extra-Marital*: Sampath and Shanthi, the actress	Untouchability

”	9. *The Financial Expert* (1952)	*Husband and wife*: Margayya and his wife	*Father and son*: Margayya and Balu *Mother and son:* Margayya's wife and Balu	*Husband and wife*: Margayya's brother and his wife *Brother and brother*: Margayya and his brother	Caste system
”	10. *Waiting for the Mahatma* (1958)	*Grandmother and grandson*: Sriram and his grandmother *Lovers*: Bharati and Sriram			Caste system Harijans and Untouchability
”	11. *The Guide* (1958)	*Mother and son*: Raju and his mother *Extra-marital*: Raju and Rosie *Guru-disciples*: Raju and the people	*Husband and wife*: Marco and Rosie	*Uncle and nephew*: Raju and his maternal uncle The jointfamily of Velan	Caste system
”	12. *The Man-Eater of Malgudi* (1961)	*Husband and wife*: Nataraj and his wife	*Extra-marital*: Vasu and Rangi, the devadasi girl		
”	13. *The Vendor of Sweets* (1967)	*Husband and wife*: Jagan and Ambika *Father and son*: Jagan and Mali	*Husband and wife*: Mali and Grace	*Mother-in-law and daughter-in-law*: Ambika and the mother of Jagan	Caste system
”	14. *The Painter of Signs* (1976)	*Lovers*: Raman and Daisy	*Aunt and nephew*: Raman and his aunt	*Husband and wife*: Andal and her husband	

4. Kamala Markandaya	15. *Nectar in a Sieve* (1954)	*Husband and wife*: Rukmani and Nathan *Parents and children*: Rukmani, Nathan and their children *Mother and daughter*: Rukmani and Ira		*Elders and the young*: Nathan and his sons *Brother and sister*: Selvam and Ira	
”	16. *Same Inner Fury* (1956)		*Husband and wife*: Premala and Kit *Lovers*: Meera and Richard		
”	17. *A Silence of Desire* (1960)	*Husband and wife*: Dandekar and Sarojini *Parents and children*: The children of Dandekar and Sarojini	*Guru-disciple*: Sarojini and the faith healer		
”	18. *Possession* (1963)		*Mother and son*: Valmiki and his mother Valmiki and the English woman, Caroline Bell		
”	19. *A Handful of Rice*		*Husband and wife*: Ravi and Nalini Thangam and her husband Appu and the mother of Nalini		
”	20. *The Coffer Dams* (1969)			*Extra-marital*: Helen and the tribal man	

,,	21. *The Nowhere Man* (1972)		*Husband and wife*: Srinivas and Vasantha *Mother and son*: Vasantha and her sons	*Husband and wife*: Vasantha's son and the English wife	
,,	22. *Two Virgins* (1973)		*Sister-sister*: Saroja and Lalitha *Husband and wife*: Amma and Appa of Saroja and Lalitha	*Aunt and nieces*: Alamelu and Saroja and Lalitha *Lovers*: Gupta and Lalitha	Caste system
5. Balachandra Rajan	23. *The Dark Dancer* (1958)	*Husband and wife*: Krishnan and Kamala *Parents and children*: Krishnan and his father and mother	*Extra-marital*: Krishnan and Cynthia (the English woman)		Caste system
,,	24. *Too Long in the West* (1962)		*Husband and wife*: Nalini and Raman *Father and daughter*: Nalini and her father		Caste system
6. Raja Rao	25. *Kanthapura* (1938)	*Mother and son*: Narasamma and Moorthy		*Lovers*: Moorthy and Ranga	Untouchability discussed at length

5.2. Analysis of the Aspects of Significant Relationships

We can infer from this chart that relationships may be broadly classified into two categories: family and community. Family relationships consist of the following: husband and wife, parents and children, brothers and sisters, mother-in-law, son-in-law and daughter-in-law, grandmothers, uncles and aunts. It is significant to note that in all the twenty eight novels analysed, the grandfather is not mentioned even as a secondary character. The community relationships include age, occupation and caste. We would observe the following in our discussion: Relationship is a form of identity and security in South India. There are very special relationships such as the son-in-law, daughter-in-law and mother-in-law. Age is a framework of relationship in which the society demands respect to the elders. Caste is a form of relationship that gives security to people rather than considered as a bondage. The challenge to caste in novels usually comes from outside the depressed and low castes.

5.3. Relationship—A Form of Identity and Security

Relationship is a form of identity and security because it gives the person the certitude of not being rejected in spite of whatever the person does. Chandran in R.K. Narayan's *The Bachelor of Arts* comes back home after messing up his life when his attempt to marry the girl Malathi ends in failure. His parents are ever willing to accept him. He is encouraged by the words of confidence from his father: "I should certainly have done something if I hadn't heard from you for some weeks more. It was only your mother was very, very worried."[1]

Nathan, the husband of Rukmani (Kamala Markandaya, *Nectar in a Sieve*) has the confidence in his wife to admit his infidelity and still be accepted by her. When Rukmani discovers his relationship with Kunthi, her neighbour, Nathan says: "I am the father of her sons. She would have told you and I was weak."[2] What gives strength to Nathan to reveal his past to Rukmani is his relationship with her. Though he has wandered, he could come back home. Dandekar is not able to live without Sarojini (Kamala Markandaya, *A Silence of Desire*). He feels the withdrawal of Sarojini in his life. He seems to feel deprived of the security he had in his life: "He wanted her back not because he desired her or to care for the children or to keep house as she had once done . . . but because above the sum of all these parts was something else, a spiritual ingrowing which made it impossible for him to be whole so long as any part of her was missing."[3]

The English teacher Krishnan finds his relaxation and security in his beloved wife Sushila (R.K. Narayan, *The English Teacher*). She almost serves as a springboard for his life, actions and sharings. "We spent an hour or more, sitting there and gossiping. She listened eagerly to all the things I told her about my college, work and life. Though she hadn't met a single person who belonged to that world, she knew the names of most of my colleagues and the boys and all about them. . . . She took sides with me in all my discussions and partisanships and hated everyone I hated and respected anyone I respected."[4] Krishnan's wife provides the form of identification he wants. The wives provide a form of security and emotional support to their husbands. Their roles as housewives and mothers give them the unique opportunity to become embodiments of relationship.

Ramaswamy, the hero of Raja Rao's *The Serpent and the Rope* recalls the death of his mother and the feeling of being an orphan and the deprivation of security that he found in his mother: "I know, my mother Gauri is not dead and yet I am an orphan."[5] He feels the same when he is informed of his father's serious disease of apoplexy and the approaching death. "Sap in me, the continuity in me was strained, was being broken. I could be an orphan again." (54)

When Ramu's wife Janaki (Venkataramani, *Murugan, the Tiller*) informs him of the conception of a child and feels within himself the continuity and security of his life. "Paternity to him was the same as immortality."[6]

In the brother-sister relationship, there is security. Ira, the daughter of Rukmani finds in her brother Selvam a symbol of confidence and trust (Kamala Markandaya, *Nectar in a Sieve*). In the words of Rukmani, "Selvam and Ira had always been close. The years of separation when my daughter went to her husband having affected their relationship not at all . . . he in turn accepted her love and returned it in his own way, deep quiet way. He understood her well better than I did who was her mother." (128) The same confidence in a brother-sister relationship is reflected in the dialogue between Saraswathi and Ranga in Venkataramani's *Kandan, the Patriot*.

Ranga: Sarasu, forgive me for these many years of silence and neglect. I feel it now a crime. I haven't written to you these years.

Saraswathi: A brother's love is brother's love with or without pen and ink and postage. It is enough you have remembered me. Not a day passed without my thinking of you and of our dear father and mother.[7]

Whether it is the relationship between husband and wife, parents and children, brother and sister, it gives a form of identity and security and provides wholesomeness and honour as it has been illustrated by the above examples from the novels.

5.4. Special Types of Family Relationships

There are very special types of family relationships peculiar to South India such as mother-in-law, son-in-law (Mapillai), the daughter-in-law and the husband's family. These relationships have their own norms of behaviour and code of conduct. The son-in-law holds a unique place of honour in the family. He is respected especially by the mother-in-law. As Krishnan, the English teacher remarks in R.K. Narayan's *The English Teacher,* "My mother-in-law was brought up in a social condition where she had to show extreme respect for a son-in-law and so she never came before me or spoke to me." (91) This same attitude of the mother-in-law regarding the son-in-law is confirmed by the testimony of Koni, the narrator of the novel *Chronicles of Kedaram:* "My mother-in-law was old-fashioned and to her a son-in-law was a being to be seen and not spoken to."[8] The presence of a daughter-in-law in a joint family affects the relationships in the family. It is depicted vividly by R.K. Narayan in *The Vendor of Sweets.* The presence of Ambika, the wife of Jagan changes the entire situation in the family of Jagan. 'At home Jagan spent very little time with sister, mother or brother, as he used to, but shut himself in and awaited his wife's arrival. But she had her share of duties in a large joint household. It would be unseemly for a daughter-in-law to seek her husband's company when the others were busy in the house in various ways. Ambika often enough reminded Jagan of her obligation as a daughter-in-law but he was blind to everything except his own inclinations. . . . His mother often commented, 'A son is a son until the wife comes' feeling bitter that he could spare so little time for others at home. His younger sister said, 'Who may you be, stranger? We have forgotten your face.' And his wife herself often said, 'please don't create all this embarrassment for me. At least pretend that you are interested in others.''"[9]

It is important to notice that these special types of family relationships peculiar to South India are handled effectively by the novelists like R.K. Narayan and K. Nagarajan who have lived all their lives in South India. They exhibit an intimate understanding of these special relationships.

5.5. Community Relationships

Hospitality to guests and strangers is considered as an essential and fundamental predictable relationship in community. "Hospitality was a marked virtue of the Tamil's from times of old. . . . Inviting them warmly, they used to share their food with the guests. Even those guests who arrived late at night were offered food and lodging."[10] In the universally acclaimed classic *Thirukkural,* hospitality is the hallmark of a good householder. "The only purpose, of a family life of virtue and wealth is to command the means of extending hospitality to guests."[11]

In Raja Rao's *The Serpent and the Rope,* the hero Ramaswamy recalls the words of his father about hospitality. "As father said, they who come will eat rice and dhal-water if we can give them nothing better; and sleep on a mat if I cannot spread them a bed in velveteen." (241)

Margayya, the hero of *The Financial Expert* (R.K. Narayan) is overwhelmed by the hospitality of the priest when he goes to consult him about the ways to become rich quickly. The priest held up a plantain and a piece of coconut for Margayya. "Probably you are hungry. Eat these. I will give you a tumbler of milk."[12] Thus hospitality becomes a fundamental and predictable relationship in community. This could be experienced in every home in South India irrespective of the economic status as it could be seen in the families of Nathan, a poor farmer (Kamala Markandaya, *Nectar in a Sieve*), Ravi, a poor urban worker (Kamala Markandaya, *A Handful of Rice*), the rich families of Margayya (R.K. Narayan, *The Financial Expert*) and Swami's father (R.K. Narayan, *Swami and Friends*) and the family of Jagan and Ambika (R.K. Narayan, *The Vendor of Sweets*).

Age is a framework of relationship in which the society demands respect to the elders. The respected one has a certain age which includes experience and authority. Age governs the language used to address the elders and the outward manifestations of respect. Respect is expressed through convincing gestures. Moorthy, the young man (Raja Rao, *Kanthapura*) meets Sadhu Narayan and when the Sadhu give him the blessings, "Moorthy falls at his feet and holds them in grateful respect."[13] Moorthy pays his respect also to Sankar, an elder of the village. Moorthy's lips tremble and he falls at Sankar's feet, but when Sankar lifts him up, Moorthy says, "No, brother you are my elder and a householder." (125) The children respect their parents and always wish for their blessings in anything they do. Rukmani recounts the attitudes and the action of her two sons Arjun and Thambi (Kamala Markandaya, *Nectar in a Sieve*) when they leave home to work in the plantations in Ceylon. "They left at first day light, each carrying a bundle with food in it and each before he went kissed Nathan's feet and then mine and we laid our hands on them in blessing." (72) Chandran (R.K. Narayan, *The Bachelor of Arts*) though he loves Malathi, the daughter of Krishna Iyer, wants his parents to negotiate the marriage proposal out of respect for them. "He would have done a number of other things, but he didn't for the sake of his parents; he wanted everything to be done in the correct, orthodox manner."[14] Respect to elders and tradition is vital in many South Indian households.

The conflict between the elders and the young is handled by Kamala Markandaya in *Two Virgins*. Respect to elders and listening to their counsel by the young is championed by aunt Alamelu. "I know what is going on these days, these days young people think they know best, they have no respect for anything except their wilful ways."[15] The young people should be left free to manage their lives without any interference from the elders is articulated by the father of Lalitha and Saroja. "Our young people have a right to lead their own lives, he cried, are they to be deprived of their rights at the whim of mindless bigots like you [Aunt Alamelu]." (176-77) In this novel one could feel the western influence on the novelist Kamala Markandaya, because of the many years spent abroad. There is an obvious contrast between R.K. Narayan and Kamala Markandaya in their perception of South indian cultural value of respect to elders based on age and experience.

Caste

We cannot discuss meaningfully relationships in community without paying sufficient attention to the factor of caste seriously. "Caste largely determines the function, the status, the available opportunities as well as the handicaps for an individual."[16] Andre Beteille observes, "Caste may be defined as a small and named group of persons characterised by endogamy, hereditary membership and a specific style of life which sometimes includes the pursuit by tradition of a particular occupation and is usually associated with a more or less distinct ritual status in a hierarchical system. . . . The English word 'Caste' corresponds more or less closely to what is locally referred to as Jati or Kulam."[17] Thus caste in South India is not merely a social structure of stratification of society but a vital factor that determines relationships in a community. Caste is a form of relationship that gives security to people rather than bondage. Even the sociologists admit the aspect of security in caste system. "The caste system survived because of two basic sociological reasons: firstly, to the upper castes it provided a convenient instrument of exploitation without endangering social stability and thus ensured their prolonged domination. Secondly, to lower castes it provided a means of security."[18] Western perception emphasizes to large extent the aspect of bondage not the security and identity provided by the caste system especially to the people of lower castes.

We cannot think of a community in a village or a town in South India without caste distinctions. Even in metropolitan areas,,one may not notice overt external marks of caste system as in a village but there is certainly a network caste system in political and economic activities. Social mixing between various castes in big towns is more accidental than a conscious effort to break down the barriers. This is the reason when we look at the chart of The Aspects of Significant Relationships on pages 98 to 102, almost all the novelists selected for our study refer to the caste structure in their novels. In fourteen of the novels there is detailed reference and discussion about the various castes interacting with one another and relationships being determined by caste. Hence it is beneficial to have a closer look at the factor of 'caste' in the novels under the following aspects: (i) The Presence of caste, (ii) Pollution, Untouchability and Exploitation, (iii) Protest to Caste coming from Outside, (iv) Caste Providing Security.

(i) The Presence of Caste

The presence of caste is depicted vividly by the novelists. The clear cut division of the village into various quarters, divided according to the castes is portrayed by Raja Rao in *Kanthapura.* The narrator of the novel, the old woman says, "Till now I've spoken only of the Brahmin quarter. Our village had a pariah quarter too, a Potter's quarter, a weavers' quarter and a Sudra quarter." (7)

Grace, the wife of Mali, a woman from America (R.K. Narayan, *The Vendor of Sweets*) confesses to Jagan, the father of Mali, "I had heard so much about the caste system in this country." (63) Krishnan (Balachandra Rajan, *The Dark Dancer*) is struggling to accept the love of Cynthia while rejecting his wife Kamala. In that struggle, he remembers the Brahmin caste to which he belongs and its exalted nature: "He was a Brahmin, a priest by heredity . . . he was the knowledge that completed power, the incarnate force in the social order to which both king and warrior turned for counsel."[19] Thus the presence of caste and its influence penetrates deeply into life's important decisions.

The presence of the 'Untouchables' the lower castes in Akkur is portrayed poignantly by K.R. Venkataramani in *Kandan, the Patriot.* "Nandan, Mookan and Katteri: Irullan, Karuppan and Irullappan—this struggling army of workers had not a square inch of ground in all the wide spaces on earth either for home or for field, but toiled on with sweat on brow in the narrow ruts of an ancient system now ploughed to deep mire by modern economic forces . . . they showed the gaiety of princes in the toddy-shop." (5) In this novel, the author looks at the struggle for survival of the lower castes in the broader context of Indian freedom struggle especially in Tamilnadu in the beginning of this century.

The existence of caste system especially the lower castes is perceived differently by various characters in Kamala Markandaya's *Two Virgins.* The removal of filth and dirt is the job of the pariahs in the village: "Amma [the mother of Saroja and Lalitha] said the pariahs should do it, it was their job, they were used to handling filth, but now-a-days they were getting above themselves. Appa said 'Remember what Gandhiji taught, they are the children of God, why should they do all the unpleasant jobs but Aunt Alamelu cries out. It is their Karma, their fate, Brother, which rendered him speechless.'" (39)

(ii) Pollution, Untouchability and Exploitation

Pollution as the effect of caste distinction is treated by many of the novelists. Pollution, by its very nature, has got to do with the types of services the lower castes perform in the village, e.g. the removal of human corpse and the animal carcass and the consumption of the animal flesh especially of the cow and other animals, the removal of filth and excrement (the scavenging work). These types of services that are so essential to the well-being of the community defile the people who perform it. The concept of pollution also originates in religious awareness of the purity of the deity which is real and present in the village. This practical and existential awareness leads to untouchability. Untouchability is not to be looked at as an isolated institution but it is a way of life reflecting the rituals of the community. Untouchability is concerned with the physical presence and the denial of access: access to common drinking water well, burial ghats, community centre, community meetings and pathways. The status of a member of a low caste is a status of penance because it is linked with the religious belief of the acquisition of merits and demerits in previous births. Hence, the Harijan by being a Harijan is doing penance not only for himself but also for the whole village and the community.

Pollution and untouchability become consistent concerns and preoccupations of the novelists. The novelists being Brahmins present pollution and untouchability from a Brahminic point of view without criticism or evaluation. The agreement or disagreement of these novelists to this type of social discrimination does not transpire clearly in the novels. It is presented in a matter of fact fashion as a vital factor affecting the relationships in the community.

Raja Rao's *Kanthapura* grapples with the problem of pollution and untouchability as one of its central concerns. Moorthy, the hero of the novel visits the pariah quarter in the village. It creates a stir in the village and people speak of pollution. "We shall be dead before the world is polluted." (13) ". . . in our village there is no Brahmin who has drunk of our holy Himvathy's water and wants caste pollutions." (40) Venkamma cries out against Narsamma, the mother of Moorthy. "If he does not stop mixing with the pariahs, this very hand—do you hear? this very hand will give him two slaps on his cheeks and one on the buttocks and send him screaming to his friends, the pariahs." (53) The fear of Moorthy being excommunicated because of his mingling with the low castes looms large in the mind of his mother. "Oh! to have a son excommunicated! Oh! to have gone to Benares and Rameswaram and to Gaya and to Gokurna and to have a son ex-communicated: I wish I had closed my eyes with your father instead of living to see you polluted. Polluted! Go away you pariah." (57-58) She becomes hysterical when she sees a Harijan Bedayya passing through the street of the Brahmins. "She grew so violent with pariah Bedayya because he would not stand aside to let her pass by, that she spat on him and shouted at him and said it was all her son's fault, that he had brought shame on her family and on the community and on the village." (58) Moorthy carries the body of the Harijan Puttaya's wife and the Brahmins denounce him: "he even carried the body for a while and when everybody saw him doing this openly—for it was on the river path mind you—they all cried 'Oh! he's lost!' (61) Even Moorthy who wants to overcome pollution and do away with untouchability as a follower of Gandhi revolts internally when pariah Rachanna's wife quickly sweeps a corner and spreads for him a wattle mat, but Moorthy confused blurts out: "No, no, no, no" and he looks this side and that and thinks surely there is a carcass in the back yard, and it's surely being skinned and he smells the stench of hide and stench of pickled pigs and the roof seems to shake and all the god and all the manes of heaven seem to cry out against him and his hands steal mechanically to the holy thread and holding it, he feels he would like to say, "Hari-Om, Hari-Om." (102) The Harijans have a separate well in the village. This is referred to in *The Serpent and the Rope* (Raja Rao). "The pariah may have his separate well and the woman slave for men." (60)

Koni, the chief character in *The Chronicles of Kedaram* (K. Nagarajan) who wants to improve the lot of the Harijans but would not like them to enter his house: "I am all for improving the lot of the Harijans and the downtrodden classes but to let them walk into our houses, that was the limit. I felt polluted." (146) The Harijans were denied entry into the temples. The violent reaction to the entry of the lower castes into the temples at the beginning of the century is recorded in *Chronicles of Kedaram* (K. Nagarajan): "They were proposing to throw all Hindu temples open to Harijans. Hindu society was rocked to its foundations." (240) "They had their deities, the Harijans, their Veerans, Irulans and Katteris who inhabited trees and stones and running streams, why should they be allowed to defile our temples?" (242)

The effect of associating with the untouchables is social ostracization. This is evident in the remark of Jagan's sister in her letter to Jagan in *The Vendor of Sweets* (R.K. Narayan): "We are ashamed to refer to you as a brother. Even when you joined Gandhi and lost all sense of caste, dining and rubbing shoulders with untouchables, going to jail and getting up to all kinds of shameful things. . . . I can hardly call you a brother in the presence of my in-laws." (137-38)

The untouchables lived outside the village to avoid pollution. This fact was resented by Gandhi when he visited one of the South Indian villages in *Waiting for the Mahatma* (R.K. Narayan): "an untouchable class they lived outside the town limits, beyond, Nallappa's Grove, where nobody went and they used only a part of the river on its downward course."[20] Ponni, the untouchable woman rescues Savitri, the Brahmin woman from the river and invites her to come to her home. Savitri declines the offer, in R.K.Narayan's *The Dark Room*: "I see you are a Brahmin and won't stay with us. I will ask someone of your own caste to receive you."[21] Srinivas (R.K. Narayan, *Mr. Sampath*) is surprised at the orthodox behaviour of his wife who wants to bathe before taking any food. "He knew that it was rigorous upbringing, fear of pollution of touch by another caste, orthodox idiocies—all the rigorous compartmenting of human beings."[22]

The evidences cited above from the novels chosen for our study show us the prevalence of the practice of untouchability born of the concept of pollution. The novelists R.K. Narayan, K.S. Venkataramani, Raja Rao and K. Nagarajan are Brahmins. They picture untouchability without discussing the moral implications of it in the Tamil society.

The Harijans not only suffer social discrimination by means of untouchability, they are also exploited. Exploitation assumes different forms. They do not have the right to organize themselves. They cannot defy the existing authority. They are denied lawful wages. They cannot own land. Their economic and social mobility is curtailed. Exploitation leads to a low self-image on account of the practical recognition of their limitations. They cultivate the self-image which the upper castes want to promote. The Harijans resent inwardly the sad situation in which they live but they cannot articulate the resentment as a group. All these problems are treated by some of the novelists chosen for our analysis.

The Harijans cannot own land. It is unthinkable. When Ramu leaves the land to Murugan to cultivate in Venkataramani's *Murugan, the Tiller,* the people of the village especially the women of the upper caste comment on the action of Ramu: "Lucky days for Pallees and Padayachis and bad ones for Brahmins. . . . Why does a Padayachi or Palli want to own lands?" (121) Murugan expresses this same feeling to his wife Ponni: "No Pallee or Padayachi owns an acre of land nor does he know where his food for the morrow will come from." (113) The untouchables do not own the land. They work for their masters belonging to the upper castes and are denied due wages. This scene of injustice is depicted forcefully in *Kandan, the Patriot* (K.S. Venkataramani): "straggling army of workers [Nandan, Mookkan and Katteri, Irullan, Karuppan and Irullappan] had not a square inch of ground in all the wide spaces on earth either for home or for field, but toiled on with sweat on brow in the narrow ruts of an ancient system now ploughed to deep mire by modern economic forces." (5) "Our wages go to the feeding and fattening of rich idle folk . . . the harvest we raise with so much of hard work we've no share in it." (13)

The life of an untouchable is an unending story of exploitation. Katteri in *Kandan, the Patriot* narrates the experiences in anger and pain and justifies the excessive drinking of toddy by the low castes: "A pot of toddy is the only friend the pariah has the world over. Have we milk or honey, fruits or flowers or any of the dainties that go to feed our ruling folk. Have we an inch of ground for home or field? Even our wedded wives are but our master's farm servants; our darling child is the shepherd boy of the pannai roaming over mud and mire, stones and thorns tending the cows whose milk goes only to feed another . . . what is pariah's life worth but for a pot of toddy?" (7) Karuppan echoes the same sentiments of Katteri (K.S. Venkataramani, *Kandan, the Patriot*): "it's better to starve and die than to work in this wretched pannai (farm) where cattle are better housed and cared for than men." (9-10) R.K. Narayan describes the visit of Mahatma Gandhi to the colony of the sweepers and the wretched condition in which they live in *Waiting for the Mahatma:* "The Mahatma entered his hut. This was one of the dozen huts belonging to the city sweepers who lived on the banks of the river. It was probably the worst area in the town and exaggeration even to call them huts; they were just hovels, put together with rags, tin-sheets and shreds of coconut mating."[23] The self-image of the Harijans is dictated to them by the upper castes. They are so much dependent on the upper castes that they believe this image to be true. The daily labourers in the estate in *Kanthapura* (Raja Rao) worship the Sahib who gives them the job. "They all rose up like one rock and fell on the ground saying 'you are a dispenser of good, O Maharaja, we are the lickers of your feet.'" (67)

Protest to caste system especially the exploitation of the Harijans comes from outside. It does not spring from the community of Harijans. The social discrimination against the untouchables is challenged by Moorthy, a Brahmin (Raja Rao, *Kanthapura*). When the Swamy threatens to ex-communicate Moorthy from the community for his association with the Harijans, Moorthy bursts out: "let the Swami do what he likes. I will go and do more pariah work. I will go and eat with them if necessary. Why not? Are they not men like us." (59) Moorthy exhorts the Harijans and fosters in them a sense of unity and equality. "Brothers . . . whether Brahmin or bangle-seller, pariah or priest, we are all one, one as the mustard seed in a sack of mustard seeds equal in shape and hue and all." (170

Chandran, a brahmin boy falls in love with Malathi and wants to marry her even without knowing her caste. (R.K. Narayan, *The Bachelor of Arts*) He reasons for himself: "A marriage would not be tolerated even between sub-sects of the same caste. If India was to attain salvation, these watertight divisions must go—community, caste, sects, sub-sects." (97) Inter-caste marriage is a form of protest against caste system as it is shown by R.K. Narayan. Though Chandran does not marry Malathi at the end, protest is present at least at the level of thinking. Kandan, the educated young man from the city is needed to awaken the Harijans of Akkur and wean them away from the destructive habit of drinking (K.S. Venkataramani, *Kandan, the Patriot*). Kandan speaks to the Harijans: "I find life in our Tamil land, mean and dirty and wretched beyond measure of words. In spite of all my active work for a year and more, you haven't improved a jot." (33) It is the same story in *The Chronicles of Kedaram* where a sensitive woman like Nirmala puts her heart and soul to uplift the Harijans and to protest on their behalf. She takes Vanchi Sastri to the Harijan colony and he acknowledges her contribution to this awakening process: "I did not see it until Nirmala took me one day and showed me the buffaloes and human beings inhabiting the same shed. We had grown callous and it needed someone like Nirmala to shake and startle us into a realisation of the stark realities." (277)

The novelists like R.K. Narayan, K.S. Venkataramani, K. Nagarajan have been part of the village culture in Tamilnadu. They are able to perceive this significant fact that the Harijans themselves are incapable of protesting for their rights. They need 'outsiders' to champion their cause especially from the upper castes. As far as the Harijans themselves, they consider caste as a form of security. They appear to be happy in their lot—maybe that is the only means of suppressing their helplessness. We have the classical example of Murugan (K.S. Venkataramani, *Murugan, the Tiller*) articulating this feeling to Ramu: "It is the order that we should labour for you. Each is meant for his own work." (58) The above novelists being Brahmins give us an upper caste perception of the factor of caste affecting the relationships in the community.

Thus, relationship remains a core cultural value in South India because it manifests itself in the following ways as we have seen in this chapter. It provides identity and security to the individual. There are special types of family relationships like the son-in-law, daughter-in-law, mother-in-law. It is seen in their respect given to the elders because of their age and experience. Relationship in the community exhibits itself in the caste distinctions. The problems of pollution and untouchability and the vehement protest from outside the lower castes to this inhuman situation, portray the structures of relationship in the community.

NOTES

1. R.K. Narayan, *The Bachelor of Arts* (Chicago: The University of Chicago Press), p. 188.
2. Kamala Markandaya, *Nectar in a Sieve* (New York: Signet books, 1954), p. 90.
3. Kamala Markandaya, *A Silence of Desire* (New York: The John Day Company, 1960), p. 214.
4. R.K. Narayan, *The English Teacher* (Mysore: Indian Thought Publications, 1955), p. 38.
5. Raja Rao, *The Serpent and the Rope* (New York: Pantheon Books, 1963), p. 6.
6. K.R. Venkataramani, *Murugan, the Tiller* (London: Simpkin, Marshall, Hamilton, Kent, 1927), p. 235.
7. K.R. Venkataramani, *Kandan, the Patriot* (Madras: Svetaranya Ashrama, 1934), p. 163.
8. K. Nagarajan, *The Chronicles of Kedaram* (Bombay: Asia, 1961), p. 97.
9. R.K. Narayan, *The Vendor of Sweets* (New York: Viking Press, 1967), p. 159.
10. M.K Mangalamurugesan, *Sangam Age* (Madras: Thendral Pathippakam, 1982), p. 189.
11. S.M. Diaz, *Aphorisms of Valluvar* (Madras: International Society for the Investigation of Ancient Civilizations, 1982), p. 58, Kural No. 81.

12. R.K. Narayan, *The Financial Expert* (New York: Noonday Press, 1964), p. 28.
13. Raja Rao, *Kanthapura* (London: Oxford University Press, 1963), p. 124.
14. R.K. Narayan, *The Bachelor of Arts* (Chicago: The University of Chicago Press, 1980), p. 135.
15. Kamala Markandaya, *Two Virgins* (New Delhi: Vikas, 1983), p. 82.
16. A.R. Desai, *Rural Sociology in India* (Bombay: Popular Prakashan, 1969), p. 18.
17. Andre Beteille, *Caste, Class and Power: Changing Patterns of Stratification in a Tanjore Village* (Berkeley: University of California Press, 1965), p. 46.
18. N.K. Sarkar, *Social Structure and Development Strategy in Asia* (Delhi: People's Publishing House, 1978), p. 9.
19. Balachandra Rajan, *The Dark Dancer* (Westport, USA: Greenword Press, 1970), p. 124.
20. R.K. Narayan, *Waiting for the Mahatma* (Mysore: Indian Thought Publications), p. 90.
21. R.K. Narayan, *The Dark Room* (New Delhi: Orient Paperbacks, 1976), p. 90.
22. R.K. Narayan, *Mr. Sampath* (Mysore: Indian Thought Publications, 1956), p. 35.

The Role of Myths and Puranas

6.1. The Importance of Myths and Puranas

The earlier chapter highlighted the aspect of the social expression of the cultural values such as the idea and role of womanhood and the significance of relationship. Myths and puranas reflect the literary and traditional aspects of the life of the people. They form part and parcel of the life and consciousness of the ordinary people in South India. Why do people use them in their day-to-day life? People use Myths and Puranas because they constitute a form of communication of shared knowledge. Everyone in the group knows the story. The people share the common cultural denominator which is the story. The stories they remember and recount are often about people who become models and examples either for good or for evil. The example has authority. Thus myths and puranas become authoritative and powerful in a community.

Myths enhance the power of tradition. They appeal to the emotions of the people. Traditional societies like the one in South India use myths and puranas to support an argument, to explain a contemporary situation because the myths exist as something real. The validation of the present takes place through the traditional as we find it in the lives of the deities, mystics, rishis, avatars, saints and godly persons. Myths form part of the tradition and education of the people in the community. Majority of the myths are narrated and handed down by the older people to the younger ones in the community. The process of education goes on.

Myths represent a form of secret discussion. Only those who form part of the culture are able to enter into discussion. The "Sthala Purana"—the myth and the story peculiar to a particular place is central to the life of the people, living in that locality. This type of localization and democratization excludes all strangers. The "Sthala Purana" becomes the source of identity. It communicates the ever present sense of reality. History and tradition are fused together in the Sthala Purana. Hence to call myths as "superstition" is ethnocentric. It is due to the lack of knowledge of the world view of the people of a particular culture and its specificity.

The influence of myths on the lives of the people is wide ranging. This is expressed emphatically by R.K. Narayan in *Mr. Sampath*: "Our epics undoubtedly are a veritable storehouse of wisdom and spirituality. They contain messages of eternal value and applicable to all times, irrespective of age or sex and so on."[1]

People are the repository of myths. It is referred to in *The Vendor of Sweets* (R.K. Narayan): "do you know that our ancestors never even wrote the epics? They composed the epics and recited them and the great books lived thus from generation to generation, in the breath of the people."[2]

Meenakshi Mukherjee describes the impact of myths and puranas on the people. "Children in India grow up absorbing the legends of the land. The public recitation of tales from the *Ramayana* pointing out its contemporary relevance is even now a living tradition . . . the Indian epics offer a widely accepted basis . . . for the collective unconscious of the whole nation."[3]

The role of myths and puranas in the lives of the ordinary people could be summarized as follows: the myths and puranas constitute the collective unconsciousness of the people and a form of communication of shared knowledge and tradition; they are the primary instrument and method of interpretation, application and participation in shared knowledge; they are expressions of intuition of a transcendent reality; people draw sustenance and inspiration from them in their day-to-day life; the myths and puranas serve as intellectual stimulants at the folk and popular level; they have a therapeutic value for the rejuvenation of hope.

6.2. The Testimony of Western Anthropologists

The Western anthropologists have stressed the vital role of myths in the lives of people. "The English word *myth* comes from the Greek *muthos* (word or speech). . . . A myth is an expression of the sacred in words; it reports realities and events from the origin of the world that remain valid for the basis and purpose of all that is. Consequently, a myth functions as a model for human activity, society, wisdom and knowledge."[4] "Myths reveal the structure of reality and the multiple modalities of being in the world."[5] Myth is "a complex cultural reality"[6]; a story or tradition which claims to enshrine a fundamental truth or inner meaning about the world and human life; contrary to popular belief, myths are not childish stories nor mere pre-scientific explanations of the world nor are myths to be equated with falsities or fantasies. Myths are deeply serious insights about reality.[7]

6.3. The Selected Novelists

It is obvious that the novelists chosen for our study cannot ignore this significant and powerful dimension of the life and culture of the people in South India. They have incorporated into their novels, myths and legends. They have used myths and puranas not merely as a literary style, but as writers who are attuned to the aspirations of the people and this significant dimension of culture. This is evident to a large extent in the case of authors like R.K. Narayan and K.R. Venkataramani who have lived most of their lives with the people in South India. Raja Rao is acutely conscious of this dimension in all his novels.

6.4. The Existing Studies

The use of myths and puranas by the Indian English novelists has been studied by many critics. The chief among them are P. Lal, Samares Sanyal and Meenakshi Mukherjee. P. Lal insists on the importance of the knowledge of myths for the Indian writer in English: "No Indian writer, in English or any of the other Indian languages, should commit pen to paper until he has spent ten years of his adult life carefully pondering the Indian classics, learning the Indian tradition and absorbing the Indian myth."[8] Samares Sanyal comments on the necessity enjoined on the English writers to use myths consciously or unconsciously. "The epics and the puranas are among the few common links which constitute an all India frame of reference. Since Anglo-Indian writing has its roots in India, the writers should have been attracted towards this rich material."[9] He analyses the uses of myths in Raja Rao and R.K. Narayan. The discussion tends to be general.[10] Meenakshi Mukherjee has suggested a frame of analysis in her book *Twice-Born Fiction*. She discusses "myth as a technique": "There seems to be two distinct ways in which myths have been used in Indo-Anglian novels: as part of disgressional techniques of which Raja Rao is the most outstanding exponent and as the structural parallels where a mythical situation underlies the whole or part of a novel." (132) In this study we shall examine the role of myths and puranas as the literary and traditional expressions of the culture of the people of South India. The tabulation on the next pages demonstrates the consistent use of myths and puranas by the South Indian novelists in English.

Three Ways of Handling Myths and Puranas

Author	Novel	Epic and Puranic Myths and Legends	Sthala Purana	Structural Parallel-Myths providing a pattern
R.K. Narayan	*The Guide*	The story of Buddha and the mustard seed (p. 17) The story of Devaka (p. 95)	The source of Sarayu in Malgudi (p. 51)	
”	*The English Teacher*	The story of great Kailas (p. 95)	The story of the Goddess Vak Matha (p. 123) [localized myth]	The story of Savitri's efforts to win back her Satyavan from the God of death (reversed)
”	*Mr. Sampath*	grand aunt—a treasure house of stories (p. 100) Shiva and the God of love and Kama (pp. 101-2) The story for the proposed film	The history of Malgudi: the passing through of Rama and Buddha (pp. 206-7)	
”	*The Man-Eater of Malgudi*	The tale of the elephant Gajendra saved by Vishnu (p. 132) Vasu, the taxidermist rakshasa (pp. 72, 174)		The myth of Bhasmasura (p. 73)
”	*Swami and His Friends*	grandmother of Swami: the story of Harichandra (p. 23)		
”	*The Financial Expert*	The story of Markandaya (p. 27) Milk and the Goddess of Lakshmi (p. 29) The story of Kubera (p. 29) The story of Saraswati and Lakshmi (p. 41) The story of Gora Kumbar (p. 61)		The story of Kannaki, Kovalan and Madhavi

”	*The Vendor of Sweets*	The Visvarupa (p. 143) Kalidasa (p. 28)		
”	*The Painter of Signs*	Aunt of Raman; the story of Krishna (p. 163)		Saints failing in the presence of beauty gods disturbing the rigorous and austere man through beautiful women (p. 40) Goddess Ganga and the king Shantanu of the *Mahabharata* (p. 27)
Kamala Markandaya	*Two Virgins*	The story of Krishna opening his mouth (p. 75)		
K. Nagarajan	*The Chronicles of Kedaram*	Viswamitra and Maneka (p. 79)	The local legend Lord Subramania made a home for himself Ilanjanaad (p. 172) Valli and Deivanai Murugan (p. 124) Sthala Purana (p. 38) Kedareswari (p. 38)	
K.S. Venkataramani	*Kandan, the Patriot*	A squirrel's little service for bridging the sea: a myth from the *Ramayana* (p. 106) The Kurukshetra (p. 174) Veena and J. Saraswathi (p. 83)		

Raja Rao	*Kanthapura*	Harikatha (part of the life of people) (p. 11) myths with contemporary situation (p. 14) The birth of Gandhi Myth mingled with the cry of freedom (pp. 15-17) The story of Prahlada (p. 90) Rama and Anjanaya (p. 108) Myth mingled with freedom struggle (p. 258) Suras and asuras	Sthala Purana of Kanthapura (p. 116) Sage Bhagiratha's penance (pp. 116, 123) The Goddess Kenchamma (p. 88) The river Hemavathy (p. 8) Sthala purana of the deeds of Moorthy	Rama-Ravana, the struggle of independence Gandhian struggle against the British (p. 126)
"	*The Cat and Shakespeare*	Myth of Shiva and the bilba tree (p. 7) Bhima and Hanuman (p. 34)	Shiva and Bhavani (p. 12) Pandya waterfall (p. 33)	
"	*Comrade Kirillov*		The story of Kanyakumari (p. 123)	
"	*The Serpent and the Rope*	The story of Yagnavalkya (p. 169) The story of Radha and Krishna (p. 379) The story of Satyavrata (p. 379) The story of Rama and Sita (p.182) The squirrel building roads (p. 181) The story of Ramadevi, the Princess of Avanti (pp. 121-23) The story of Lord Buddha (p. 296) The grandmother Lakshamma	The city of Hyderabad (p. 245) The Gangetic plain (p. 33)	Ravana and Rama—India and the British Rule (p. 181)

6.5. Three Ways of Handling the Myths and Puranas

It is clear from the above tabulation that the novelists chosen for our study have used myths and legends to a great extent in the following three ways.

1. They have interspersed and fused the epic and puranic myths and legends into the story of the novel as a part of the narrative. They have used myths to explain a contemporary situation, to highlight a character in the novel, to justify the position of a character, to elaborate a viewpoint. They have represented the consciousness of the people in South India authentically and affirmed the cultural value of these myths.
2. Myths have provided the Sthala Purana—a peculiar phenomenon of localization in South India in the novels. "The feature that most conspicuously distinguishes the Tamil myths from the classical corpus of Sanskrit myths is the persistent localization of the mythic action. *Sthala Puranas*, as collections of stories that have clustered around individual shrines and their environments are by definition repositories of localized myths and legends."[11] The novelists especially R.K. Narayan and Raja Rao have taken this phenomenon of localization in their novels seriously.
3. At times, myths and puranas provide the pattern and the framework for the novel as a whole.

We will examine in detail the three ways in which the novelists have used the myths and legends and how these myths are part of the culture and consciousness of the people in South India.

6.6. Analysis

6.6.1 Fusion of the Myths and Legends into the Narrative

The myths and legends are fused into the narration of the story of the novel. It is done spontaneously and naturally by novelists like R.K. Narayan. Myths become part of the narrative. Myths are introduced to explain and justify a contemporary situation. When people come to Raju, the supposed spiritual guide of the people in *The Guide* (R.K. Narayan), he narrates to them a story from the life of Buddha, of the woman who went in search of a handful of mustard seeds from a home where death was unknown. Raju tells his attentive listeners: "If you show me a person without a problem, then I'll show you the perfect world."[12] Raju justifies the generous offering of the people, the basket of edibles that they would be blessed by God as in the case of devaka who begged for alms at the temple gate every day and would not use any of his collections without first putting them at the feet of God. (17)

Krishnan gets encouragement and support by remembering the myth of Lord Shiva, sending a piece of Kailas, laden with ice to reduce the heat of the world, when he is taking care of his wife Sushila, suffering from high fever in *The English Teacher* (R.K. Narayan). Krishnan is inspired to write a poem comprising this myth: "This great Kailas in one mound of Ice where Shiva and Paravati sport, which catch the gleam of ethereal lights, heavenly Rainbows; Here for us, God has sent a piece of Kailas down to subdue the Mercury Column."[13]

Sampath, Srinivas and Somu are considering themes and stories for their film to become popular instantaneously with the audience. Somu tells Sampath and Srinivas the tremendous power of the myth in *Mr. Sampath* (R.K. Narayan): "Krishna Leela the boyhood of Krishna and his friends, up to his killing of the demon Kamsa—I was talking to my grand-aunt, you know how our people are a treasure-house of stories and she mentioned these stories one by one."[14]

The significant detail to be noted to this allusion is the fact that the myths are part and parcel of the culture of the people. The old people could say these stories just from memory. Myths have a perennial cultural value to the people. Srinivas and his friends choose the story for the proposed film: the episode of the Lord Shiva and the God of love, Kama. Somu and Sampath are listening to Srinivas in rapt attention to the story : "Shiva is in a rigorous meditation, when his future bride Parvati, is ministering to his needs as devotee and an absolute stranger. One day, opening his eyes, he realizes that passion is stirring within him and looking about for the cause, he sees Kama, the Lord of Love, aiming his shaft at him. At this, enraged, he opens his third eye in the forehead and reduces Kama to ashes." (101)

Nataraj wants the elephant of the temple to be saved from Vasu, the taxidermist, in *The Man-Eater of Malgudi* (R.K. Narayan). He remembers the elephant Gajendra rescued by Vishnu and draws strength from this religious myth that Vasu will not be able to harm the elephant: "the tale of the elephant Gajendra, the elephant of mythology who stepped into a lake and had his leg caught in the jaws of a mighty crocodile; and the elephant trumpeted helplessly, struggled, and in the end desperately called on Vishnu, who immediately appeared and gave him the strength to come ashore out of the jaws of the crocodile." "In this story," I told myself, "our ancestors have shown that an elephant has a protected life and no one can harm it."[14] Here myth is used to articulate a religious belief and to affirm the sacredness of the temple elephant. Vasu is depicted as a rakshasa. The friend of Nataraj, Sastri sketches the character of Vasu: "He shows all the definitions of a rakshasa . . . and went on to define the make-up of a rakshasa or a demoniac creature who possessed enormous strength, strange powers and genius but recognized no sort of restraints of man or of God." He said, "Every rakshasa gets swollen with his ego. He thinks he is invincible, beyond every law. But sooner or later something or other will destroy him. He stood expatiating on the lives of various demons in *puranas* to prove his point." (72) "He had to conserve all that might for his own destruction. Every demon appears in the world with a special boon of indestructibility. Yet the universe has survived all the rakshasas that were ever born. Every demon carries within him unknown to himself, a tiny seed of self-destruction and goes up in thin air at the most unexpected moment. Otherwise what it is to happen to humanity." (173-74) Here the reference to the ancient myth of Bhasmasura is used to portray the character of Vasu and to justify and legitimize his death. The contemporary situation is explained through these allusions to mythology. The grandmother is the repository of myths and legends in *Swami and Friends.* She impresses on Swami, the need for a life of truthfulness: "begged leave to start the story of Harischandra, who just to be true to his word, lost his throne, wife and child and got them all back in the end."[15] This story expresses the validity of a life of truthfulness and the sacrifice that goes with it. R.K. Narayan is reminded of his own grandmother who used to entertain him with myths and stories.

The Financial Expert (R.K. Narayan) is strewn with myths. The priest persuades Margayya to perform a particular Puja to defeat death and disease, highlighting the story of Markandaya: "the boy devotee of God Shiva, destined to die the moment he completed his sixteenth year. When the moment came, the emissaries of Yama (the God of Death) arrived in order to bind and carry off his life, but he was performing the Puja—the dark emissaries could not approach him at all! Markandaya remained sixteen to all eternity and thus defeated death . . . it's that very puja I am performing on behalf of the child (crippled with a disease from childhood) who is much better for it."[16] The performance of a particular ritual is justified through a myth. The priest uses the myth to convince Margayya about the efficacy of the Puja. The priest offers a tumbler of milk to Margayya. He does not like milk. The priest takes exception to the behaviour of Margayya, pushing away the tumbler of milk with the back of his hand. The priest exhorts him about the greatness of milk: "Milk is one of the forms of Goddess Lakshmi, the Goddess of wealth. When you reject it or treat it indifferently it means you reject her. She is a Goddess who always stays on the tip of her toes all the time, ever ready to turn and run away. There are ways of wooing and keeping her. When she graces a house with her presence, the master of the house becomes distinguished, famous and wealthy." (29) Margayya swallows the entire story. His gullibility is exploited by the priest. He touches the tumbler reverently and respectfully and drinks the milk, taking care not to spill even a drop. The priest applauds his action and comes out with another story from the *Mahabharata*: "the story of Kubera, the wealthiest man in creation, who undertook a long arduous penance as atonement for spilling a drop of milk on the floor of his palace." (29)

Margayya wants to become rich and wealthy. The priest tells him to pray to Goddess of wealth Lakshmi, "you would propitiate Goddess Lakshmi, the Goddess of wealth. When she throws a glance and it falls on someone, he becomes rich, he becomes prosperous." (41) The priest talks about the conflict between Lakshmi and Saraswati, the deity presiding over knowledge and enlightenment: "When Saraswati favours a man, the other Goddess withdraws her favours. There is always a rivalry between the two—between the patronage of the spouse of Vishnu and the spouse of Brahma . . . you are one of those for whom both are fighting at the moment." (41) The myths are used here for instruction and the simpleton Margayya is manipulated by the priest to do his bidding.

Balu, the son of Margayya kicks away his plate of rice. Margayya is very angry. He shouts at his son: "If you kick away your rice, I will kick you." The boy bursts into tears. The wife of Margayya is reminded of "the story of Gora Kumhar, a potter who was devoted to the God Vishnu and took no care of his family. At meal times, his little son demanded ghee like Balu. . . . The Lady went out to borrow ghee from the next house, leaving the child in the care of the father who was stamping on wet clay all the time. When she was gone, he got into a mystic ecstasy and started dancing and did not notice the child crawling under his feet and when the mother returned with ghee, the child had been stamped into the wet mud. Margayya's wife burst into tears, remembering this story, which she had seen as a drama in her young days." (62) The above story is a good illustration of myth mingling with the life-situations of the people. One cannot but admire the ease with which R.K. Narayan brings in the myths into his narratives, thus manifesting his rootedness in the culture of the people.

Savitri and Ramani go for a film in *The Dark Room* (R.K. Narayan). The novelist describes the impact, the film about Krishna, made on her: "Savitri like the majority of those in the hall, knew the story, had heard it a number of times since infancy, the old story from the epics, of Krishna and his old classmate Kuchela, who was too busy with his daily prayers and meditation to work and earn and hence left to his wife the task of finding food for their *twenty children* . . . Krishna's boyhood, he had his gawky classmates waylaying curd-sellers and gorging themselves. . . . An endless procession of rustic women with pots on their heads passed under the trees, in the branches of which a gang was waiting; the women halted under the trees nearly asked to be robbed of their pots. How they wrung their heads at the broken pots and chased Krishna."[17] The novelist brings out the familiarity of the people with the myth of Krishna and how it is part and parcel of their collective unconsciousness.

Jagan in *The Vendor of Sweets* (R.K. Narayan) is unable to understand the muti-faceted character of his son Mali. He remains a puzzle to Jagan. Jagan was reminded of the concept of *Viswarupa* that he read about in the *Bhagavad Gita:* "When the warrior Arjuna hesitated to perform his duty on the battlefield, God came to him in the guise of his charioteer and then revealed Himself in all His immensity. On one side He was thousand faced." (143) Jagan is discussing with his cousin regarding the incomplete education of Mali. The cousin is referring to Kalidasa who never went to a college. Jagan uses the myth of Kalidasa's poetic creation in contempt: "College or no college, I know Kalidasa was a village idiot and a shepherd until the Goddess Saraswati made a scratch on his tongue and then he burst into that song, Syamala-dandakam, and wrote his *Sakuntala.*" (28) Myths form part of the daily conservations of the people. R.K. Narayan illustrates this through the character of Jagan.

Aunt of Raman visited the temple in the evenings and did not wish to miss certain important episodes in Krishna's life. Aunt spoke to him of the story, she had heard in the evening: "Do you know when Krishna revealed himself to the maidens every one of them, thousands of them, felt convinced that Krishna was there dancing with them. . . . How it was achieved, the pundit explained."[18] R.K. Narayan points to the custom of religious myths being expounded in the temples, in the evenings for the benefit of the old as well as the illiterate. The oral tradition of transmitting myths continues even today in South India.

The myth of Krishna is very popular with the South Indian novelists. Kamala Markandaya alludes to one of the aspects of this myth in *Two Virgins.* Amma and Appa were quarrelling over Lalitha and her future and the indulgences given to her that have led to her downfall in getting herself entangled with Mr. Gupta, the film producer. Saroja, the younger sister of Lalitha, entrusts her to Lord Krishna: "God is good, she said and one must have faith in his boundless wisdom and she told them the story of the little boy who was in reality, God incarnate who had opened his mouth and revealed to astounded onlookers the world entire."[19] The myth expresses the deep faith in the divine in times of stress and strain.

Vasu's softness for Nirmala Chari and his involvement with her is debated by Vanchinatha Sastri and Koni, the narrator of the novel in *Chronicles of Kedaram* (K. Nagarajan). Vachinatha Sastri is a man of the world and he expresses the hold of Nirmala on Vasu by referring to this myth: "He quoted Viswamitra and Maneka and other classical examples to support this book that when a beautiful woman stoops to folly, the man concerned cannot hold out for long."[20] The myth is used by the novelist to strengthen the argument of a character and to justify a contemporary situation.

Rajee comments on the contribution of Kandan to the independence struggle in Tamilnadu in *Kandan, the Patriot* (K.S. Venkataramani). She refers to the popular myth from the *Ramayana* of the service of a squirrel to Rama to bridge the sea between Sri Lanka and India. "He wrote to me that he was coming home to his Tamil land for social and political work, some little selfless deed for his fellow men, a squirrel's little service for bridging the sea as he put it."[34] This is again an instance of using a popular myth to explain a contemporary situation.

The habit of reading the myths and puranas of ancient India especially the *Mahabharata* by housewives like Neelakshi is mentioned in the same novel. "Neelakshi having failed to persuade Raghu to dine, herself took a copy of the *Mahabharata* and opened the volume where the great fight of Kurukshetra begins . . . Neelakshi too stopped pouring over the battle scenes of the *Mahabharata* which kept harmony with the tumult of her heart and ambitions." (174) The myths provide solace and comfort to the troubled hearts.

The enchanting power of music elevated to mythical dimension in *Kandan, the Patriot.* When Saraswati plays the Veena and begins to sing, it is an ecstatic experience to listen. This is described by Sundaram, her husband: "In the height of ecstasy when music lived with the brooding silence and charmed the solitude, a long, long shining cobra came winding along the veranda with raised head and spreading hood deeply fascinated by and lost in music. The milk in the pot bubbled its own joy. The cat saw the shining cobra as if in a dream. But it moved not forgetting in the spell, the ancient feud of the race. The instinct to strike and its native venom in the role of music." (83)

Raja Rao has used myths and legends in his novels for various purposes. He refers to the custom of singing *Harikatha*—the story of God in *Kanthapura.* The Sastri, the Harikatha exponent kept the people hanging on his lips. Raja Rao explains this in a footnote. "Harikatha—literally story of God. Generally a story from one of the Indian legends is taken and with music and dance the Harikatha—performer relates it in extemporized verse. Sometime the music and dance stop and he explains the whole thing in familiar prose."[22] The story of Parvati winning Siva is used to explain a contemporary situation: "Siva is the three—eyed. Swaraj too is three-eyed. Self-purification, Hindu-Muslim unity, Khaddar. He talks of Damayanti and Shakuntala and Yashoda and everywhere there is something about our country and something about Swaraj." (14) Myth mingles with reality at the hands of the Harikatha exponent. Gandhi is compared to Krishna in *Kanthapura:* "You remember how Krishna, when he was but a babe of four, had begun to fight against demons and had killed the serpent Kali. So too our Mohandas began to fight against the enemies of the country . . . more and more men followed him as they did Krishna, the flute-player and he goes from village to village to slay the serpent of the foreign rule." (14) Moorthy feels intensely the presence of the divine in his life and remembers the story of Prahlada who felt keenly the presence of Hari in his life. This reference is in *Kanthapura:* "He remembered the child Prahlada who had said Hari was everywhere and he said to himself, 'I shall see Hari too.'" (90-91) When Moorthy invites the pariah Rachanna to join him in the freedom struggle, Range Gowda ridicules the invitation by alluding to the myth in the *Ramayana (Kanthapura).* Here the myth is used for satire and ridicule. "Every Rama needs an Anjanayya and he's your fire-tailed Hanuman and they all laugh." (108) The whole of the independence struggle is envisaged as the conquest of Rama over Ravana: "They say the Mahatma will go to the Red-man's country and he will get us Swaraj. . . . And Rama will come back from exile and Sita will be with him, for Ravana will be slain and Sita freed." (258) Skepticism about the real change in India after independence is expressed by some of the villagers in a sarcastic way and a myth is used as a vehicle of sarcasm. "All this is very good, but if the white men shall leave us tomorrow, it will not be Rama-rajya we shall, but the rule of the ten-headed Ravana." (126) Raja Rao uses the techniques of mingling myth with reality to provide a mythical context to the whole of independence struggle. He highlights the character of shared knowledge of myths especially the myths from the *Ramayana.* Myths are used to explain the significance of contemporary situation.

Ramakrishna Pai in *The Cat and Shakespeare* wishes the blessings of God in his life. When he looks at the stump of a bilva tree, he rembers the myth: "It's a scraggy tree but dear to Shiva, for one night a hunter trying to shoot at his game . . . went up this obnoxious stump and in his hours of waiting sent down leaf after leaf and Shiva image being beneath, Shiva himself came in a vision and said: Here I am."[23] Here the myth is used to validate the religious belief. The good native of

Govindan Nair and his helping tendency is brought out by this myth of Bhima and Hanuman in *The Cat and Shakespeare:* "He loved because of his big heart. . . . He was like Bhima. . . . You want the flower of Paradise? Hanuman himself will help. . . . (Bhima a hero of the *Mahabharata* is helped by Hanuman, a figure in the *Ramayana,* to find the flower of Paradise)." (34)

The Serpent and the Rope (Raja Rao) abounds in myths and legends from the puranas. In this novel, the myths are used to expound philosophical truths. The ideal relationship between Savithri and Ramaswamy is compared to the relationship of Yagnyavalkya and his wife, in the words of Ramaswamy: "Savithri proved that I could be I . . . I could not possess Savithri I became I. Hence the famous saying of Yagnyavalkya to his wife: 'The husband does not love the wife for the wife's sake, the husband loves the wife for the sake of the self in her.'"[24] The philosophical truth of world as maya, an illusion is illustrated by the moving story of Radha and Krishna in which Radha takes food to the sage Durvasa, crossing the flooded river Yamuna. Krishna educates her: "My Lord, she answered, 'the river believes you are a brahmachari and after all who should deny it better than me, your wife?' And then I go to Durvasa and he eats with his palm going down his gullet and he says, 'Tell the river, Durvasa who is ever in upavasa asks you to open and let Radha pass.' And the river opens herself, makes a way large as a village pathway and I pass over to this side. The world is a fib, a misnomer, a lie. 'The world, my dear, is not a lie, it is an illusion' replied Krishna." (380) Harichandra told the truth and lost his kingdom and his wife, but he found the truth. He narrates the story of Satyavrata: "He who has taken the vow of truth." Satyavrata wants to save the deer from the hunter. He gives an evasive reply and utters the profound Vedantic truth: "He who sees cannot say and he who says has not seen." (347) The myth is used to explain the nature of truth in India. The devotion of the little mother to Rama is conveyed through the story of Ishwara Bhatta who went on a pilgrimage to Benares. He told his wife and son Brahma Bhatta to repeat the story of Rama every Saturday. They fail to do so. Disaster comes to the household of Ishwara Bhatta. He comes back and redeems the house from ruin and tragedy. (248-53) The consciousness of the myth and its usage is illustrated by the story told by the little mother so vividly. Ramaswamy explains the meaning of *Dharma* to Swanston. Dharma comes from the word *dhru,* to sustain, to uphold. It is as it were the metaphysical basis of our world insofar as the world exists, of course. The law of Dharma is seen in the fair, pregnant Sita sent away because the populace questioned her integrity. By sending Sita into exile, the kingdom of Ayodhya was perpetually righteous. (181-82) Raja Rao has used the myths judiciously and elaborately to convey profound philosophical truths.

The numerous examples cited above substantiate the first way in which the selected novelists have used myths and legends in their works of fiction. They have mingled the myths into the narrative to explain a contemporary situation, to highlight a character, to justify the position of a character, to elaborate a viewpoint, to be satirical, to communicate profound philosophical truths. The collective unconsciousness of the people of South India emerges in the novels beyond any doubt.

6.6.2 The Sthala Purana

The strong regional cultural element of South India is articulated by the widespread reference to sthala purana by the selected novelists. It is peculiar phenomenon of localization of the myth in South India. R.K. Narayan, K. Nagarajan and Raja Rao refer to this peculiar phenomenon in South India in their novels.

The source of the river Sarayu that passes through the village of Velan where Raju, the Guru is staying. Someone had gone to the spot where the river originates. There was a small shrine on the peak right at the basin. The one who had gone to the spot gives an accurate description of this sthala purana to Raju in *The Guide* (R.K. Narayan): "It must be the source of Sarayu mentioned in the mythological stories of Goddess Parvati jumping into the fire; the carving on one of the pillars of the shrine actually shows the Goddess plunging into the fire and water arising from the spot." (51)

Krishnan is taken by the priest to a temple and he describes the significance of the temple through the localized myth in *The English Teacher* (R.K. Narayan): "The Goddess. It is said that Sankara when he passed this way built it at night, by merely chanting her name over the earth and it stood up, because the villagers asked for it. The Goddess is known as Vak Matha, the mother who came out of a syllable." (123)

The locus of most of the novels of R.K. Narayan is Malgudi. Malgudi is given the pride of place as a town with special importance because Rama and Buddha have passed through this town. The Indian myths about Rama and Buddha are localized in *Mr. Sampath* (R.K. Narayan) when the history of Malgudi is recounted. (206-7)

Margayya in *The Financial Expert* (R.K. Narayan) is taken by the priest to the little temple at the end of Vinayak Mudali street in Malgudi. There under a cracked dome was an inner shrine containing an image of Hanuman, the God of Power, the son of wind. The priest describes the localized story: "According to tradition this God had pressed one foot on the very spot where the shrine now stood, sprang across space and ocean and landed in Lanka, there to destroy Ravana, a king with ten head's and twenty hands, who was oppressing mankind and had abducted Rama's wife Sita." (27)

The local legend of Lord Subramania making a home for himself in Ilanjanad is referred to by Koni, the narrator in *Chronicles of Kedaram* (K. Nagarajan): "The local legend is that the Lord Subramania, the martial son of Parameswara happened to come here on one of his punitive expeditions and being charmed with the country round, made a home for himself there. That is said to have brought peace and prosperity to the countryside." (172) Religion becomes an ever present reality to the inhabitants of Ilanjanad and the localized myth expresses the ardent faith and deep religious belief of the people: "It was enchanted country, the domain of the Lord Subramania who watched over the neighbourhood from his shrine on Ilanja hill. . . . The seven hamlets over which he ruled were collections of tumble-down, mud-and-thatch huts, all within hailing distance of one another and inhabited, it was credibly alleged, by descendents of two families who had come down with God Subramania himself in the distant past when he alighted, astride his peacock mount, his brides, Valli and Deivanai, by his side, on Ilanja hill. . . . Subramania was locally known as Ilanji Velavan and from his peacock throne under which nestled his faithful servitor, the five-headed cobra, he looked after his people and their crops and kept their cattle safe from the rinder-pest and the murrain." (124)

Raja Rao uses the sthala purana in an effective manner in his novels. In *Kanthapura,* the sthala purana of the village Kanthapura in which the Gods visit the village (116), sage Bhagiratha made his penance in Kanthapura (123), the Goddess Kenchamma is the Goddess of the locality (88) and the river Hemavathy which is the locus of the deeds of the hero Moorthy. (8)

The river Bhavani has a secret tryst with Lord Shiva and one shudders at the beauty and silence of the river in *The Cat and Shakespeare.* Govinda Nair speaks of this relationship: "Look, look, there Shiva comes down three days before full moon and in Marghashira to sport himself with his spouse Bhavani. The river therefore carries flowers and the young tigress cubs." (12) The description is graphic and life-like. The story of Kanyakumari is an excellent example of a sthala purana. "When Parvati was tired after she had crossed the Krishna, the Godavary and the Cauvery, she reached this spot—the rock of India. . . . Parvati had set her heart on the great God Shiva. She was not able to marry. . . . Unmarried, she ever awaits the marriage that will never take place. Shiva in disgrace went back he weeps. He woos her from the Himalayas. She has not changed her mind. At the tip of India stands Parvati, she is India." (*The Cat and Shakespeare*)

The story of the city of Hyderabad is connected with the Goddess Lakshmi and Hassan Qutub Shah who killed his prime minister for the sake of the Great Lady of the Lotus. He built her a temple with four spires, as though it were a mosque: "She resides with us, the Goddess does to this very day. . . . She shines on our coins, does Lakshmi, as Bhagyavathi and that is why we call our city Bhagyanagar city of beautiful wealth, for Hyderabad is but a vulgar homonymn."[25] This sthala purana is narrated by Raja Rao in *The Serpent and the Rope*.

The sthala purana is specific to South India in most cases. It is linked with the deities and their exploits. The abode of the Gods and Goddesses is localized. The sthala purana has a religious flavour. The selected novelists have used this in a creative way in their novels, thus highlighting the strong regional cultural element of South India.

6.6.3 The Structural Parallels

Myths provide the pattern and the framework for the novel as a whole. R.K. Narayan in *The English Teacher* uses the story of Savitri's efforts to win back her Satyavan from the God of death. Krishnan tries to contact his dead wife Sushila through a medium. One can easily discover links with the story of Savitri's efforts to win back her Satyavan from the God of Death (Yama) but the roles of the husband and wife are reversed here.[25] In *The Dark Room* (R.K. Narayan) one could glean the link between the story of Kannaki and Kovalan and his mistress Madhavi and the story of Savitri who tries to liberate herself from the cruelty of her husband who has a mistress in his office. The plot of the novel, *The Man-Eater of Malgudi* has a structural parallel in the myth of Bhasmasura. The image of Vasu is based on the following principle: "The evil must destroy itself." Vasu, the taxidermist fits into the definitions of a Rakshasa. Sastri compares very accurately Vasu with demon Bhasmasura: "Bhasmasura who acquired a special boon that everything he touched should be scorched while nothing could ever destroy him. He made humanity suffer. God Vishnu incarnated as a dancer of great beauty, named Mohini: the asura became infatuated with her and she promised to yield to him if he imitated all the gestures and movements of her own dancing. So a dance began: the demon was an accomplished one; at one point of the dance, Mohini placed her palms on her own head and the demon followed this gesture in complete forgetfulness and was reduced to ashes that very second, his blighting touch becoming active on his own head." (73) The same happened to asura of Malgudi—

Vasu, who struck himself on the forehead, defending himself from mosquitoes and killed himself.[27]

The relationship between Daisy and Raman in *The Painter of Signs* (R.K. Narayan) is based on the associative understanding of the legend about king Shantanu and Goddess Ganga from the *Mahabharata,* when Daisy wants to have her own way, Raman promises to be like the ancient king Shantanu. To understand the relations between Daisy and Raman, it is necessary to recollect the following legend: "Shantanu was fond of hunting and passed much of his time in the woods. One day when he was wandering along the banks of the Ganges he saw a lovely maiden. He fell in love with her and wanted her to be his wife. She agreed to be his wife but did not want him to interfere in anything that she did. The king agreed. Eight children were born to them. But those children as soon as they were born, were one after another thrown into the river by Ganga. When the king tried to prevent the killing of the eighth child, the wife left him."[28] Daisy leaves Raman and goes away to the village leaving Raman in Malgudi. This is Narayan's interpretation of the legend from the *Mahabharata* given from the point of view of modernity, where the painter of signs, Raman plays the role of king Shantanu.

Raja Rao, in his novels *Kanthapura* and *The Serpent and the Rope* gives a mythical design to the independence struggle, the struggle of Gandhi against the British as the struggle between Rama and Ravana.[29] Thus, the selected novelists use myths to provide a pattern and framework to their novels.

The detailed analysis above indicates clearly that the selected South Indian novelists in English have taken the significant and powerful dimension of the culture and life of the people in South India, the role of myths and puranas. They have fused the myths and legends into the narrative of the novels. They have used the individual myths as part of the narrative. They have depicted the peculiar phenomenon of South India—the localization of myth through the reference to Sthala Purana. They have also handled myths to provide a pattern and framework to the novels as a whole. In all the three ways, they have affirmed the cultural value of the myths and puranas in the day-to-day life of the people.

NOTES

1. R.K. Narayan, *Mr. Sampath* (Mysore: Indian Thought Publications, 1956), p. 134.

2. R.K. Narayan, *The Vendor of Sweets* (New York: Viking Press, 1967), p. 74.
3. Meenakshi Mukherjee, *The Twice-Born Fiction* (New Delhi: Arnold-Heinemann, 1974), p. 131.
4. Kees W. Bole, "Myth—An Overview," *Encyclopaedia of Religion,* ed. Mircea Eliade, Vol. 10, p. 261.
5. Mircea Eliade, *Myths, Dreams and Mysteries* (New York: Harper and Row, 1950), p. 15.
6. Mircea Elaide, *The Structure of Myth,* p. 5.
7. Gerars A. Arbuckle, "Mythology, Revitalization and the Refounding of Religious Life," *Review for Religious*, Vol. 46,1 (Jan.-Feb. 1987), p. 14.
8. P. Lal, "Myth and Indian Writer in English: A Note," in M.K. Naik, ed., *Aspects of Indian Writing in English* (New Delhi: Macmillan, 1979), p. 18.
9. Samares C. Sanyal, *Indianness in Major Indo-English Novels* (Bareilly; Prakash, 1984), p. 162.
10. In this book, Sanyal devotes a chapter, "Myth as Technique; A Special Characteristic of Indianness" (pp. 158-201) to analyse the myths in the novels of Raja Rao and R.K. Narayan.
11. Shulman, *Tamil Temple Myths* (New Jersey: Princeton University Press), p. 4.
12. R.K. Narayan, *The Guide* (Mysore: Indian Thought Publications, 1958), p. 14.
13. R.K. Narayan, *The English Teacher* (Mysore: Indian Thought Publications, 1955), p. 65.
14. R.K. Narayan, *The Man-Eater of Malgudi* (Harmondsworth: King Penguin Books, 1983), p. 132.
15. R.K. Narayan, *Swami and Friends* (Mysore: Indian Thought Publications, 1960), p. 23.
16. R.K. Narayan, *The Financial Expert* (New York: Noonday Press 1964), p. 27.
17 R.K. Narayan, *The Dark Room* (New Delhi: Orient Paperbacks, 1976), p. 22.
18. R.K. Narayan, *The Painter of Signs* (Mysore: Indian Thought Publications, 1977), p. 163.
19. Kamala Markandaya, *Two Virgins* (New Delhi: Vikas, 1983), p. 175.
20. K. Nagarajan, *Chronicles of Kedaram* (Bombay: Asia, 1961), p. 79.
21. K.S. Venkataramani, *Kandan, the Patriot* (Madras: Svertaranya Ashrama, 1934), p. 106.
22. Raja Rao, *Kanthapura* (London: Oxford University Press, 1963), p. 13.
23. Raja Rao, *The Cat and Shakespeare* (New York; Macmillan, 1965), p. 7.
24. Raja Rao, *The Serpent and the Rope,* p. 169.
25. Shyam M. Asnani, *Critical Response to Indian English Fiction*, Ch 3, "The Use of Myth in R.K. Narayan's Novels" (Delhi: Mittal, 1985), p. 30.
26. Ibid., p. 31.
27. E.J. Kalinnikova, "Indian Myths and Legends in R.K. Narayan's Interpretation," *Perspectives on R.K. Narayan,* ed. Atma Ram (Ghazizbzd: Vimal, 1981), p. 23.
28. *Ibid.*, p. 24; R.K. Narayan, *The Painter of Signs*, p. 27.
29. *Kanthapura,* p. 126; *The Serpent and the Rope,* p. 181.

The Absorption of Native Proverbs, Expressions, Festivals and Customs

7.1. The Importance of the Subject

Another dimension of literary and traditional aspects of South Indian culture is the use of the Tamil and Kannada proverbs, expressions, festivals and customs by the South Indian novelists in English. These are fused into the narratives of the novels. This fusion illustrates the absorption of the South Indian cultural tradition into the English language. This fusion also serves as an instrument in the hands of the novelists to indigenize the English language itself. When we find these proverbs, expressions, festivals and customs strewn over the narratives, the novels become authentic self-expressions of the authors especially R.K. Narayan, K. Nagarajan, K.S. Venkataramani who have spent most of their lives in South India. Raja Rao also uses a few proverbs in his novels.

7.2. The Role of Proverbs

Proverbs are the embodiments of cultural values of the people of a given culture. They form part of the oral tradition. They are explorative and confidence-building. They are used frequently by the people in their daily lives. They simplify argument, validate action, exhibit the knowledge and collective wisdom of the people. The South Indian novelists in English cannot ignore this vital aspect of the culture of the people if they want their novels to be authentic. The use of proverbs reveals the quintessence of the shared knowledge and community experience. No significant literature can bypass it. The proverbs and expressions of the native languages provide a context for the novelists. They are used in the novels for indictment, encouragement, solace and comfort. They also serve as means of education, ridicule, satire and expression of contempt. *Tholkappium*, an ancient Tamil classic prescribes the characteristics of proverbs. They should be truthful, brief, good for the ear, full of content and softness. "The Muthumoli (proverb) is that which occurs to give expression to a particular idea with reason quoted in subtle, short, bright and easy style."[1]

Absortpion of Native Proverbs and Expressions

Author	Novel	Proverbs and Expressions
K. Nagarajan	*The Chronicles of Kedaram*	1. An only tree is not a garden nor An only son a son (p. 225) Thanimaram thopakuma? Oru Mahan Varisahuma? 2. A man should not drink milk sittting under a toddy palm. (pp. 133-34) Panai maram aruhe Palkudithalum kal entre solvarkal.
R.K. Narayan	*The Painter of Signs*	3. He began to spin a yarn. (p. 44) Avan pu sutha arambithan Kayiru thirikka arambithan Saradu vida arambithan (Tamil) Avan paruthi Neyya arambithan (Kannada) 4. When you are married to the devil, you must be prepared to climb the tamarind tree. (p. 97) Pisasai pendatiyaga kondavan puliyamaram erah changadappattal eppadi?
”	*Waiting for the Mahatma*	5. What can a little cobra do, even if you have brought it up on cow's milk. It can only do what its breeding tells it to do. (p. 119) Sirunagathirkku Pasumpall varthalum athan savahasa kunathan atharku. 6. Roams with the hare and hunts with the hounds. (p. 17) Muyalodu odi nayidu vettaiyaduvan Adummecha mathiri, thambikku prnnum ketta Mathiri.
”	*The Dark Room*	7. The difficulty that has risen before you like a mountain will soon vanish like the dew. (p. 103) Malaipol vantha thuyar panipol ningum.

,,	*The Vendor of Sweets*	8. Even if eighty million ideas float across your mind, you cannot wear more than four cubits of cloth or eat more than a little measure of rice at a time. (p. 67) Ettukkodi ennangal odinalum Ettumulat thuniyum oru alakku arisiyium tan nalaikku (Kannada). 9. Frogs in the well. (p. 49) Kinatrutu thavalai. 10. Do you think rupees, annas, pies drop from the sky ? (p. 59) Marathila kasenna kaicha thinguthu. (Tamil) Akasathilerunthu rubayahavum anavahavum paisavahavum enna kottutha. (Kannada)
,,	*The Guide*	11. I have better things to do of a morning than make a genius out of a clay-head. (p. 12) Mittalai methai akkuvathaivida kalaiyil enakku vere jilikal eralam. (Kannada)
,,	*The Man-Eater of Malgudi*	12. You may close the mouth of an oven but how can you close the mouth of a town. (p. 168) Ulai vayai mudinalum vurvayi muda mudiyuma. 13. Building a house and conducting a marriage were the two Herculean tasks that faced a man (p. 46) Vidu kattippar, kalianam pannipar.
,,	*The Guide*	14. It is written on the brow of some that they shall not be left alone. (p. 49) Silarin netriyil avarkal nirkkathiyaha vidapadamattargal entru eluthiyulathu. (Kannada) Antru avan eluthiya eluthu matriya nadakkappokirathu. (Tamil)
,,	,,	15. He asks for the car as if it were his grandfather's property. (p. 61) Avan pattan sothena ninaithu kar ketkiran. (Kannada) Intha thottam enna un pithiraja sotha. (Tamil)
,,	,,	16. What a treasure you have in your hand, without realizing its worth like a monkey, picking up a rose garland. (p. 71) Un kaiyil sikkiya puthaiyal kurankin kaiyil sikkya pumalai ahivittathe! (Kannada and Tamil) 17. An empty vessel makes much noise. (p. 212) Nirai kudam thalumbathu, kurari kudam Kuthadum. (Tamil)

,,	*The English Teacher*	18. That I should be destined to see these scenes in our life—I have never known such things in our family. (p. 109) Enkalathil intha kuthaiyellam parkkanumunnu en thalai yeluthu. Nammaa kudumbathile ipaddiellam kidayathu. (Historical precedent)
,,	,,	19. I was clinging to a grass blade at the brink of a well. (p. 170) Alkinatrin vilimbil, pullin nuniyil thongikondirunthen.
K.S. Venkataramani	*Murugan, the Tiller*	20. There is one in Tamil, Swami, the injured toe injures itself again. (p. 2) Patta kalile padum, ketta kudiye kedum.
,,	*Kandan, the Patriot*	21. Change oru Mudaliar: as well as you can wash an ass into a horse. (p. 14) Kaluthaiyaik kaluvi kuthiraiyakkalam muthaliyarai thiruthuvatha?
,,	,,	22. Stealing his steps like the cat that goes to the cheese or a spider that leaps on to the fly. (p. 18) Punai vennai thiruda nadappathaippola Silanthi irayai nokki paivathaippola.
,,	,,	23. Never go empty-handed to children. (p. 94) Kovilirukkum vittirkkum kulandai irukkum vittirukkum verunkayai visicchllalama?
,,	,,	24. Only the dog would go back again to the rubbish heap to lie down upon curling its tail. (p. 132) Valarukkappatta naithan mindum kuppaimettai nokkicchellum paduppatharku.
,,	,,	25. When the wind bows, we must glean the grain as the proverb goes. (p. 134) Katrullapothe thutrikkol.
Raja Rao	*Kanthapura*	26. Does a boar stand before a lion or a jackal before an elephant? (p. 81) Singathinmun katterumai nirkumaa yanayinmun onai valattuma? 27. One cannot stitch up the mouths of others. (p. 136) Urar vayaai usipottut thaikka mudiyathu. 28. Police are not uncle's sons. (p. 251) Maman vittuppillaikal illai, Policekararkal.
,,	*The Serpent and the Rope*	29. The temple needs a bell and the girl a husband to make the four walls shine (The little mother). (p. 274) Kovilukku maani vendum. Pennukku kanavan vendum. Nalu suvariyum thulanga vaikka.

The proverbs and expressions found in the selected novels are given in the above chart. This section of the chapter would analyse the cultural implications and values embedded in the usage of the proverbs and expressions.

7.3. Proverbs and Expressions in the Selected Novels

Proverbs and expressions from native languages are freely used by the novelists for various purposes. We will look at this literary phenomenon authorwise to highlight their insertion and involvement in their own culture.

K. Nagarajan in *Chronicles of Kedaram* has used a Tamil proverb to express a compliment through the narrator of the novel, Koni. Koni compliments Charu on her pregnancy and her husband Vasu: "We have a homely saying in Tamil that an only tree is not a garden nor an only son, a son."[2] In the same novel, narrator Koni takes Vasu to task for having friendship with Nirmala Chari who is not his wife. This relationship is the talk of the town. Koni wants to remind Vasu of his reputation being at stake and gently gives him an indictment and advice: "I reminded him of the homely Tamil saying that a man should not drink milk, sitting under a toddy-palm." (133-34) One could feel the distinct native touch in Nagarajan.

R.K. Narayan in many of his novels has fused the proverbs into the narrative. He shows himself to be an artist who could use the proverbs and expressions both from Tamil and Kannada. In *The Painter of Signs,* Raman tries to justify the use of glasses for his eyes to his girl friend Daisy with whom he is madly in love. He is unable to give a proper and convincing answer. Therefore to avoid embarrassment he starts giving her false reasons. At this juncture, R.K. Narayan uses this proverb with an ironic touch: "He began to spin a yarn."[3] This proverb is found both in Tamil and Kannada.

In the same novel, Daisy, the girl friend of Raman spends a night on the top of the tree to avoid the amorous advances of Raman when they have to spend a night alone on their way to a village in a bullock cart. She uses this proverb sarcastically to indicate her narrow and prudent escape from Raman: "When you are married to the devil, you must be prepared to climb the tamarind tree." (97) These proverbs illustrate the avoidance of the situations of embarrassment.

In *Waiting for the Mahatma,* the old aunt of Sriram loses all her spirit and zest for life, from the time police had come looking for Sriram because of his involvement in the independence struggle. The Old Aunt validates her action of bringing up Raman and justifies it for herself:

"What can a little cobra do even if you have brought it up on cow's milk. It can only do what its breeding tells it to do." (97) Mahatma Gandhi had come to the village of Sriram and he wants to talk to the people. Natesh, the Municipal Chairman, becomes his interpreter and translator. The school master in the crowd listening to Gandhi murmurs this proverb to disapprove the opportunism of Natesh with a touch of irony: "Runs with the hare and hunts with the hounds." (97)

Ponni, in *The Dark Room* (R.K. Narayan) rescues Savitri from drowning. Savitri is depressed and wants to end her life because of her husband's ill-treatment. After saving her from her attempt to commit suicide, Ponni, a low caste woman blesses with all her heart, Savitri of the high caste: "God will protect you. The difficulty that has risen before you like a mountain will soon vanish like the dew."[5] This beautiful Tamil expression is used appropriately by R.K. Narayan to bring in auspiciousness, good luck, assurance and God's blessings.

Jagan, the vendor of sweets, in *The Vendor of Sweets* (R.K. Narayan) refutes his cousin with this expression in Tamil, who suggests to him to make money and build mansions. This expression reflects the collective wisdom of the people of South India and as an alternative to human greed and insatiable desire: "And what would one do with many mansions . . . even if eighty million ideas float across your mind, you cannot wear more than four cubics of cloth or eat more than a little measure of rice at a time."[6] Jagan is surprised at the ignorance of the adjournment lawyer about America whereas he is in a better position to know about it because of his son Mali. He uses this Tamil expression to reveal his contempt and annoyance: "How presumptuous of the man to talk of America, while he was there to provide first hand information! People's notions were fixed. Stupid fellows. Frogs in the well." (49)

Swami needs a lot of things for his examination like clips, pad, pen, paper and ink. (R.K.Narayan, *Swami and Friends*) He hesitates to ask these things from his father because he is mortally afraid of him. The father of Swami is surprised at this list. He used a common idiom found both in Tamil and Kannada to express his surprise: "What preposterous list is this? Do you think rupees, annas and pies drop from the sky?"[7] R.K. Narayan makes use of this native idiom, to express irony and satire in his very first novel.

The two Tamil proverbs that appear in *The Man-Eater of Malgudi* (R.K. Narayan) reflect the collective wisdom and shared experience of the people of South India. The Press owner Nataraj tries to poison Vasu, the taxidermist through the dancing girl Rangi. The wife of Nataraj cautions him quoting a Tamil proverb: "You may close the mouth of an oven but how can you close the mouth of the town."[8] One of the regular customers of Nataraj, expresses his difficulty in getting his daughter Sushila married: "How truly have our elders said . . . he quoted a proverb to the effect that building a house and conducting a marriage were the two Herculean tasks that faced a man." (46) It is significant to note that these two proverbs are born out of the proven experience and collective wisdom of the people of South India.

The Guide (R.K. Narayan) has a few proverbs and expressions to manifest the various moods of the different characters. The father of Raju is desperate in making Raju study and goes out of the house with this remark: "I have better things to do of a morning than make a genius out of a clay-head."[9] When Raju becomes the vendor at the Malgudi railway station, he becomes the errand boy of the tourists. He resigns himself to his fate in life. He indulges in self-pity with this comment: "It is written on the brow of some that they shall not be left alone." (49) Raju's annoyance at the odd behaviour of Rosie's husband demanding all the time taxi, is revealed to Gaffur, the taxi-driver with this exasperated remark: "He asks for the car as if it were his grandfather's property." (61) The insensitivity and the lack of love of Rosie's husband for Rosie and the admiration and love of Raju for Rosie, makes him exclaim: "What a treasure you have in your hand, without realizing its worth—like a monkey picking up a rose garland." (70) Raju impresses Velan of his knowledge and wisdom by mingling proverbs in his discourse: "Have you not heard the saying—an empty vessel makes much noise." (212) Velan is in total admiration of Raju's wisdom, the pretending Guru: "How many good sentiments and philosophies you have gathered in that head of yours, Sir!" (212) R.K. Narayan fuses these proverbs and expressions into the narrative to make them look like expressions in English. The English language itself gets indigenized.

The feelings of pathos, self-pity and the sense of loss of the wife Sushila by Krishnan are echoed by the mother of Krishnan (R.K. Narayan, *The English Teacher*) in the typical Tamil expression used by R.K. Narayan: "That I should be destined to see these scenes in our life. I have never known such things in our family."[10] This comment reveals also the historical precedent in their family and it is loaded with a sense of tradition. Krishnan, the English teacher, is unable to reconcile himself to the loss of his wife. He is so depressed and his poignant emotion of sadness is manifested in a graphic Tamil expression incorporated into the text of the novel by R.K. Narayan: "I was clinging to a grass blade at the brink of a well." (170)

K.S. Venkataramani's novels are full of the native touch. He is so much immersed in the indigenous culture, he cannot but use the expressions from the Tamil language to make his novels, authentic and authoritative expressions of the culture of the people. The following examples will prove this point. Murugan, the tiller, from the lower-caste working in the lands of Ramachandran is fond of using expressions from his mother-tongue to his master (K.S. Venkataramani, *Murugan, the Tiller*): "There is also one in Tamil, Swami: the injured toe injures itself again, replied Murugan who was ever anxious for the prestige of his mother-tongue."[11] The proverb indicates the succession of sufferings in a person's life referring to the death of Ramachandran's mother and his failure in B.A. The illiterate Murugan is full of the collective wisdom of South India.

In *Kandan, the Patriot* (K.S. Venkataramani) Nallan speaks to his brother Pavadai about the impossibility of changing the outrageous and atrocious behaviour of their boss, the Mudaliar who exploits them. The following proverb makes his remark sharp, pointed and satirical: "Change our Mudaliar! as well you can wash an ass into a horse." (14) The stealthiness of Ranga in following his beloved Rajeswari and patting gently on her shoulders is described vividly by the novelist with the help of a Tamil expression: "Stealing his steps like the cat that goes to the cheese on the spider that leaps on to the fly." (18) Kandan visited the house of the untouchable Karian and the four children came crying to his knees and asked for sweetmeats and food. Kandan regretted his thoughtlessness in not bringing sweets for the children by quoting the proverb which emphasizes the propriety of bringing gifts to the temple and the children: "never go empty-handed either to the temple or to children." (94) The Oxford-educated Kandan comes to the village and works for the uplift of the poor Harijans. Sundaram, one of the inhabitants of the village comments on the revolutionary action of Kandan and the futility of his efforts. The proverb quoted manifests the despising and contemptuous attitude of the high caste for the low caste. "Only the dog would go back again to the rubbish heap to lie down upon curling its tail." (132) On the contrary Saraswati who is inspired by the patriotic zeal of Kandan appreciates the efforts of Kandan. She affirms that this is the appropriate time to work for the liberation of the country by quoting this proverb to reinforce the argument: "This is the time for work in our country. When the wind blows, we must glean the grain, as the proverb goes." (134)

Raja Rao, though he spent most of his years abroad, is aware of the necessity to sprinkle his novels with Tamil and Kannadiga expressions and proverbs to reflect the collective consciousness of the people of South India. The courage to face the police atrocities during the independence struggle of the common people especially the pariahs is alluded to by the usage of this proverb (*Kanthapura*); "Bade Khan can wave his beard and twist his moustache. What is a policeman before a Gandhi's man? Tell me does a boar stand before a lion or a jackal before an elephant."[12]

The Waterfall Venkamma assassinates the character of Rangamma, as a widow who has association with different men in the village (*Kanthapura*). Rangamma faces this embarrassing and difficult situation by ignoring the comments of the villagers by this proverb: "One cannot stitch up the mouths of others. So let them say what they like." (136) During the thick of the independence struggle, so many men are wounded by the brutality of the policemen who are derided and despised. One of the rural women uses a well-known Tamil expression to despise the police in *Kanthapura*: "the police are not your uncle's sons, are they?" (251)

The little mother in *The Serpent and the Rope* applauds the late marriage of Saroja, the sister of Ramaswamy and her happiness, with this well-known Tamil saying that ushers in auspiciousness. "The Temple needs a bell and the girl a husband to make four walls shine."[13]

Thus the novelists use proverbs and expressions from the native languages with the following cultural implications: to pay a compliment, to validate an argument; to reflect and represent the collective wisdom of the people, born out of experience; to provide satire and irony, to avoid situations of embarrassment; to give assurance; to portray the different moods and feelings of characters in the novels. R.K. Narayan, K.S. Venkataramani, and K. Nagarajan show themselves rooted in the soil of South India by this facility of integrating the proverbs into the narrative and thus indigenizing the English language itself. R.K. Narayan has a lion's share as it is evident from the above analysis. Raja Rao makes the native air breathe through his novels by the uninhibited use of native proverbs and expressions.

7.4. The Role of Festivals

The word for festival in Tamil is *Pandigai* which means celebrating the ancient, the old for the individual and community welfare. It is significant to observe the close link between these two words *Pandigai* and *Panpadu*—festival and culture. The festivals become cultural expressions of the people. They bring out the individual and communitarian relationship with the natural environment, the seasons of the year, the deities, the religious beliefs and the world-view of the people in South India. The following examples could be cited. Margali festival going with the season of winter; Chitra festival to celebrate the advent of summer; Pongal to celebrate the Benevolence of Gods for the harvest; the

South Indian Customs and Festivals

Author	Novel	Religious Customs	Festivals	Marriage	Funeral	Miscellaneous
R.K. Narayan	*The English Teacher*	Receiving the holy water from the priest (p. 70)			Funeral procession and rites (p. 105)	Welcome the daughter-in-law with arathi (p. 35) Evil eye (p. 110) Washing before studying (p. 115) Delicacy to say 'no' (p. 159)
"	*The Guide*	worshipping God (p. 11)	Tamil New Year— Dasara Deepavali (p. 79)			The need for washing and breakfast (p. 55)
"	*The Financial Expert*			Horoscope (pp. 45, 152)		you must never ask someone where or why he is going (p. 50)
"	*The Vendor of Sweets*	Tulasi plant (p. 152)		The betrothal ceremony (p. 115) Marriage (p. 157) Looking for the bride (p. 147) Penn Parthal		
"	*Mr. Sampath*			Horoscope		
"	*The Dark Room*		Navaratri (p. 24)			
"	*The Painter of Signs*					Belief in astrology (pp. 506)

”	*The Bachelor of Arts*			Horoscope (p. 130) Extensive reference to this in the novel		
Balachandra Rajan	*The Dark Dancer*					Kolam (p. 5)
Kamala Markandaya	*Silence of Desire*	Tulasi plant (p. 7)				
”	*Possession*					rahukulam (p. 26)
”	*Nectar in a Sieve*				Funeral dirges sung by women on Raja's death	Gratitude: carrying a garland of roses and jasmine to welcome him and a time for good luck
”	*A Handful of Rice*	Fire walking (p. 211)				
”	*The Nowhere Man*				mingling of the ashes in a sacred river (p. 40)	
Raja Rao	*The Serpent and the Rope*			The marraige of Saroja (pp. 269-71)		
”	*Kanthapura*	Offering ten coconuts and kumkum worship (p. 95) recitation of Gayatri Mantra (p. 59)	Kathak festival (p. 116)			
”	*The Cat and Shakespeare*		Dussera festival (p. 67)			
K. Nagarajan	*The Chronicles of Kedaram*		Thai Pushyam (p. 123) Mandagapadi during the chitra festival (p. 5)		Funeral rites (p. 189)	The temple bells ringing: sign of auspiciousness (p. 202)

Tamil New Year to usher in auspiciousness; Amman festival, the prayer to the Goddess of rain to solicit the co-operation of nature; commemorating the birth and the great exploits of the Avatars of Gods like Rama Navami, Krishna Jayanti, Vinayaka Chaturthi, Kandasasthi. It is interesting to note that there is a story behind every festival and the festivals themselves become a complex institution in South India. Every festival is connected with purification, fulfilment of a virada, pilgrimages and penances. In most of the villages in South India, they have their own *Sthala* (local) festivals to appease the deities of the villages. *Therukoothu* (street theatre) the ancient form of the people's theatre goes on the whole night. Festivals promote happiness, unity and hospitality, religiosity and piety.

The whole year, especially the Tamil Calendar is filled with festivals: Tamil New Year (Chitra) Chitra Paurnami, Vaigasi Visagam, Adiperukku; Avani Avattam, Navaratri in Puratasi; Deepavali and Kandasasthi in Iaipasi, Karthigai Theepam in Karthigai, Vaikunda Eagadasi in Margali, Pongal in Thai; Masi festival in Masi, Panguni Uthiram in Panguni.

7.5. Festivals in Selected South Indian Novelists

It is natural that the South Indian novelists make a constant reference to the festivals celebrated in South India, as indicated in the above chart. R.K. Narayan refers to the Tamil New Year, Dassehra and Deepavali. Raju, the pretending Guru in *The Guide*, knew by the gifts the disciples offered, the festivals they were celebrating: "When they brought him sweets and fruits, he knew that the *Tamil New Year* was on. When *Dassehra* came they brought in extra lamps and lit them and the women got busy all through the nine days, decorated the pillared hall with coloured paper and tinsel; and for *Deepavali* they brought him new clothes and crackers and he invited the children to a special session and fired the crackers and he invited the children to a special session and fired the crackers." (79) The villagers want to share their joy and jubilation with the Guru. This indicates the communitarian dimension of the festivals.

The Navaratri festival is alluded to in *The Dark Room* (R.K. Narayan). "In the month of September, the streets rang with the hawkers selling dolls—the earliest intimation to the coming Navaratri festival." (24) The Navaratri festival consists in decorating dolls in houses which includes the dolls of the Gods and Goddesses. This same festival is explained in Raja Rao's *The Cat and Shakespeare:* "at the end of September it was—no, in fact at the end of August, for the rains had not ended yet and the *Dussera,* not yet there."[14] The novelist gives also a footnote on the same page describing the festival: "Dussera is perhaps the most important festival of India. It takes place after the rains and lasts for ten days, during which worship is made to the elephant, horse, armour, books and the pipal tree." (67)

The Kartik festival fascinates Raja Rao in *Kanthapura*. He describes it with poetic ecstasy: "Kartik has come to Kanthapura, sisters—kartik has come with the glow of lights and the unpressed footsteps of the wandering gods; white lights from clay-trays and red lights from copper stands and diamond lights that glow from the bowers of entrance-leaves; lights that glow from banana-trunks and mango twigs, yellow light behind white leaves, and green light behind yellow leaves, and white light behind green leaves." (116) This is a clear example of the mingling of the myths, religious belief and celebration in the lives of the people.

K. Nagarajan in *Chronicles of Kedaram* makes a special mention of a typical Tamil festival which is *Thai Pushyam*: "It was *Thai Pushyam.* A saint's day, so to speak, only pushyam was a star. When the sun was in Capricorn and that was from about the middle of January to the middle of February—and pushyam the reigning star of the day—we celebrated it. All Kedaram collected on the Nilaveni sands, to the east of Kedaram, four miles away. It was hallowed ground, the meeting point of the Nilaveni and the Ganges, which was believed to travel South all the way from Benares, by an underground channel and emerge at the Sanghya, where she was supposed to meet her daughter, the Nilaveni. The exact point of meeting was known to the priests who showed it to the worshippers and to the eye of faith, the meeting of the waters was said to be visible." (123) This festival is again a meeting point of religious belief, myths and celebration. It also becomes 'Sthala' festival with a local myth. In the same novel, the novelist talks about the *Mandagapadi* i.e. the families sponsor the festivals for many generations by which the tradition is kept. The failure to observe this custom can result in serious conflict in the village. Even an outsider, an Irishman is given the privilege to participate in the *Mandagapadi.* Donovan, the Irishman, who is the collector of the district for ten years has this privilege: "He could speak Tamil like a 'native' and had his own *Mandagapadi* during the chaitra festival in Kedarnath's temple." (5)

The festival referred to in the novels indicate the communitarian dimension of the celebration, fusion of religious belief, myth and sthala purana. Thus the festivals become the cultural expressions and manifestations of the people of South India.

7.6. The Role of Customs in South India

The customs peculiar to a culture manifest the distinctiveness and specificity of that culture. The customs also give a glimpse into the ways of behaviour of the people who belong to that particular culture. The deep meaning behind each of the customs is shared only by that community. The failure to observe these customs will bring in the sanction i.e. praise or blame of the community. The South Indian novelists make their novels specific, depicting the culture of South India by their explicit reference to religious, marriage, funeral, social customs practised by the people. The list analysed here is obviously not an exhaustive one. The customs chosen here are meant to explain the strong South Indian element in the novels.

Religious Customs

R.K. Narayan in *The English Teacher* describes the custom of visiting the temple and receiving the blessings of the priest. Krishnan goes with his wife Sushila to the temple and Sushila, being a devout woman, performs this ritual: "She received the holy water from the priest and touched her lips and eyes, put a vermilion dot on her forehead and tucked the flower offered to the God in her hair." (70) The ablutions that are performed before the worship of the divine is explained by R.K. Narayan in *The Guide*. The chief character Raju even as a child observes faithfully this custom: "I washed myself at the well, smeared holy ash on my forehead, stood before the framed picture of gods hanging high up on the wall and recited all kinds of sacred verse in a loud ringing tone." (11) This religious custom is practised specially in Brahmin households even to-day in South India. The novelist being a Brahmin has a first hand knowledge of this custom.

The reference to the sacredness of the tulasi plant in South Indian households is made in *The Vendor of Sweets* (R.K. Narayan) and *A Silence of Desire* (Kamala Markandaya). When Jagan comes back to his native place from town in *The Vendor of Sweets*, he sees his sister going around the tulasi plant which is a sign of auspiciousness, divine blessing and religious devotion: "His sister was circumambulating the sacred tulasi plant in the central yard and grinned at him mischievously, while her lips were muttering prayers." (152) The sanctity of the tulasi plant is highlighted by Kamala Markandaya in *A Silence of Desire,* in the description of the house of Dandekar: "The six rooms that they rented were built around a country yard, a square of about eight feet with an uneven cement floor in the middle of which stood the divine tulasi that his wife worshipped. It was a small evergreen plant, crammed into bright and decorative brass in which it languished, surviving without health, but with a sharp, imperious smell that made you forget its looks—a smell that clung to your hands until you had washed and scrubbed, and even after, and could haunt you if you did not pray."[15]

Walking on fire during a religious festival is an important custom in South India. It is done with devotion and commitment. The excitement and wonder of this scene charged with emotion in a religious atmosphere is depicted by Kamala Markandaya in *A Handful of Rice*. It is also done as a penance and as an offering to obtain a particular grace from the deity: "a dozen men came out of the night into the full glow of the fire-bed. They were naked except for the loincloths, their bodies oiled, their feet bare, the fire walkers. There was a gasp, the mass holding-in of breath before release . . . the leader raised his head and said clearly, 'The power is thine O God, not mine' and at once with no further hesitation he stepped on to the coals and ran lightly over the glowing bed. In his wake came followers, invoking God's power as he had done, treading the same path as lightly as if those red-hot coals were flowers under their feet."[16]

Raja Rao, in *Kanthapura,* expresses the desire of Ratna to offer this special worship to the deity for the well-being of Moorthy: "'God, I shall offer ten coconuts and a kumkum worship. God keep him alive for me.' Then she rose and fell prostrate before the gods in the sanctum." (95) In the same novel, he refers to the custom of Rangamma reciting the Gayatri mantra, the prayer of blessing, to soothen her anger against Moorthy and the prayer softens her a lot: "And she sat herself down to meditate and the Gayatri muttered itself out soft and fast." (59) The novelist adds a footnote in the same page to explain this prayer: "Gayatri, the essential part of the Brahminic prayer. It runs thus: 'O face of the True Sun, now hidden by a disc of gold, may we know thy Reality and see thee face to face.'" (59) The reference to this prayer illustrates the familiarity of Raja Rao of the religious customs and practices in a Brahminic household. Himself being a Brahmin, he depicts this aspect of culture with authenticity and authority.

Marriage and Funeral Rites

The customs regarding marriage funeral rites add a distinctive touch to the novels bringing out the strong regional element. The role of horoscope in marriage is alluded to by R.K. Narayan in many of his novels. He gives an extensive treatment of this custom. Margayya in *The Financial Expert* consults an astrologer about the marriage prospects of his son. The astrologer gives him the expert opinion: "The seventh and ninth houses in your son's horoscope . . . are not quite sound. The girl's marriage possibilities are the purest. The two horoscopes cannot match—they are like soap and oil." (153) In *The Bachelor of Arts,* there is a lot of discussion concerning the marriage of Chandran by his parents with Ganaptahi Sastrigal, the marriage broker. Sastrigal expresses his firm belief in the agreement of the horoscopes of the boy and the girl: "How are we to know whether two persons brought together will have health, happiness, harmony and long life, if we do not study their horoscopes individually together." (130) In the same novel, the father of Chandran has his own apprehensions about the role of horoscope in marriage: "Why bother with horoscopes . . . personally I have no faith in them." (130) Sastrigal tries to convince him of the necessity of horoscope. The mother of Chandran narrates her own experience as a young girl: "It is the custom when a girl is ready for the marriage, her horoscope will be sent in ten directions and ten different persons will see her and approve or disapprove. . . . A year before my marriage, a certain doctor was eager for an alliance with our family, the horoscopes too matched and his son came to look at me, but I didn't like his appearance and told my father that I won't marry him." (252) Chandran is unable to marry the girl whom he likes and loves because of the ill-matching of the horoscopes. The father of the girl writes a letter to the father of Chandran to this effect: "I am returning herewith the copy of your son's horoscope, which you so kindly sent to me for comparison with my daughter's. Our family astrologer, after careful study and comparison, says that the horoscope cannot be matched. Since I have great faith in horoscopy and since I have known from experience that the marriage of couples ill-matched in the stars often leads to misfortune and even tragedy, I have to seek a bridegroom elsewhere." (142) Chandran is fed up with all kinds of formality and he reacts sharply: "To the dust-pot with your silly customs." (118) The mother of Chandran believes in all these customs and "as long as she lived she would insist on respecting the old customs." (118) The landlord who is a friend of Srinivas asks for the horoscope of Ravi to settle his grand-daughter in marriage to him in *Mr. Sampath* (R.K. Narayan): "My tenant in that portion—Ravi isn't he your friend? I have often seen him going with you. I observe all things. Why don't you persuade him to give me his horoscope? I think he will be a good match for this girl."[17]

The above instances quoted from the selected novels provide substantial evidence to the presence and practice of looking for the horoscope of the boy and the girl in settling marriages in South India.

R.K. Narayan refers to the betrothal ceremony in a Tamil household in a vivid manner in *The Vendor of Sweets* in the alliance between Jagan and Ambika. Jagan goes with his parents and brother to the house of Ambika. He is expected to behave in the best possible manner because of the solemnity and the seriousness of the occasion. This 'penn-parthal' is a special custom in South India. Jagan becomes hungry at the sight of the Jilebi (a sweet) placed in front of him in the home of Ambika: "The protocol was inflexible . . . a glance from his brother restrained him . . . they were honoured visitors, on whose verdict would depend the future of the girl. It was a highly serious and important role and they were expected to carry themselves with dignity without displaying emotion even at the sight of jilebi." (147) The betrothal ceremony is conducted in a grand manner in the house of Jagan: "The senior priest of the house, a gaunt Goldman, stood up and read the notice aloud, his voice quivering with nervousness. It was announced that Jagannath, son of so and so, was to marry Ambika, daughter of so and so, on the tenth of September, etc. etc. The father of the bride handed this important document ceremoniously to Jagan's father, together with an envelope in which he had put currency notes, half the dowry in advance." (154)

The vivid description of the marriage of Jagan with Ambika gives us a glimpse of a South Indian wedding; the feasting, the gaiety, the innocent jokes, fooling and solemnity. (157) The elaborate description of a typical wedding in a Brahmin family, the wedding of Saroja, the sister of Ramaswamy is given by Raja Rao in *The Serpent and the Rope*. The description is given as an eye-witness account of Ramaswamy: "The sacrificial fire burnt and there the ghee was poured and then the milk, the curd and the honey. Agenya Samohoam . . . svaha. . . . I threw flowers and kumkum-rice on the bridal couple . . . seven times she went round the fire making saptapadi, seven times taking the names of my ancestors . . . the fire burnt, the ghee went in, the flames purred and rose and asked for more. . . . The tali was touched by the elders first, then by the great and then by all of us. The bridegroom tied it around Saroja's neck. . . . 'She looked like a Lakshmi' said Aunt Subbakha to me." (270-71)

The funeral rites are explained with accuracy and poignant emotion by R.K. Narayan in *The English Teacher* when Krishnan's wife Sushila dies. It is a typical funeral procession that takes place in South India: "The corpse-bearers, grim and sub-human, have arrived with their equipment—bamboo and coir ropes. Near the front step they raise a small fire with cinders and faggots—this is the fire which is to follow us to the cremation ground. . . . Everyone gathers a handful of rice and puts it between her lips—our last offering. They shoulder the stretcher. I'm given a pot containing the fire and we march out." (105) The funeral dirges sung by the village women when Rukmani's son Raju dies, are described poetically by Kamala Markandaya in *Nectar in a Sieve*: "For this I have given you birth, my son that you should lie in the end at my feet with ashes in your face and coldness in your limbs and yourself departed without trace, leaving this huddle of bones and flesh without meaning."[18] Srinivas tries to mingle the ashes of his wife Vasantha into the Thames river and the policeman takes an exception to his behaviour in *The Nowhere Man* (Kamala Markandaya): "He could not help feeling with Vasantha, who in her breath and bones had remained wholly Indian. She would have liked her remains committed to the currents of an Indian river."[19] This is an explicit reference to the custom of mingling the ashes of the dear one in a sacred river.

Social Customs

The following social customs are mentioned in the selected novels. The mother of Krishnan welcomes her daughter-in-law and the child with arathi in *The English Teacher* (R.K. Narayan): "She was standing at the door way and as soon as we got down cried: 'Let Sushila and the child stay where they are.' She had a pan of vermilion solution ready at hand and circled it before the young mother and the child, before allowing them to get down from the carriage." (35) When the mother of Krishnan is leaving for her native place, she wants the child to be warded off from 'Evil eye': "She touched the child's cheeks and cracked her fingers on her temple as an antidote for *Evil Eye*." (110) This is the common belief in South India that one of the reasons for one's suffering is the evil eyes of those who cast aspersion on you and wish you ill-luck. To remove this evil influence on the child, the mother of Krishnan performs the above action. The custom of washing oneself before studying to respect the sacredness of learning is referred to in the same novel. Krishnan persuades gently his daughter to wash before studying: "We must first wash and then read stories, because it is Goddess Saraswati and we must never touch her without washing." (115) The typical South Indian custom of washing oneself before breakfast to feel fresh is explained satirically by Raju in *The Guide* (R.K. Narayan): "He must wash, change his clothes, refresh himself with idli and coffee and only then can we expect anyone in South India to think clearly on all matters of this world and the next." (55) In South India, it is not considered polite and courteous to ask someone where he is going, when someone is starting from the house. This is depicted in *The Financial Expert* (R.K. Narayan). The villager asks Margayya "'May I know why you are going this way?' Margayya said, 'You must never ask "Why" or "Where" when a person is starting out: that'll always have an adverse influence." (50) The custom of drawing 'kolum' in front of the house is found in *The Dark Dancer* (Balachandra Rajan): "He looked at the Kolum, the decorative emblem patiently drawn each morning on the water-sprinkled floor, the symbol of the universal design, giving each house its particular geometry of perception."[20] It is not advisable to undertake anything significant and noteworthy during *raukalam* in South India. This explains the unwillingness of Valmiki to start his craftsmanship in *Possession* (Kamala Markandaya): "the raukalam, the 'dark period' during which it is inauspicious to undertake anything of note, whose ramifications were ill-defined now."[21] To express one's gratitude for the favours done, it is customary to honour the benefactor with a garland of roses and a lime in South India. This is observed by Rukmani in *Nectar in a Sieve* to thank Doctor Kenny for all that he has done to her family. "I went therefore to the whitewashed cottage on the fringes of the town, expectant, carrying a garland of roses and jasmine to welcome him and a lime for good luck." (109) When the temple bells peal, it is considered a sign of auspiciousness and blessing. This is indicated by K. Nagarajan in *The Chronicles of Kedaram*: "When he took leave of his grandfather on the steps of Vanasankari Vilas, the temple bells of Kedareswar set up a rousing peal. We were all happy that the journey was blessed of Gods." (202)

The absorption of proverbs, expressions, festivals and customs from the native languages and culture by the selected South Indian novelists confirm the following: their insertion and involvement in their culture. Though they are writing in English, they cannot ignore the tremendous impact of their own culture on them; they have incorporated and integrated the proverbs, expressions, festivals and customs naturally and spontaneously into the text and narratives of the novels; this absorption adds to the richness of the English language which itself gets indigenized; the novels become authentic cultural expressions of South India with a strong emphasis on the regional element; one could glean the pervasive South Indian cultural element in the novels; the selected novelists being Brahmins themselves have a first hand idea of the elitist culture and hence most of the time, we find references to this 'great tradition'; they rarely refer to the festivals and customs of the lower castes belonging to the little tradition—folk culture and tradition.

NOTES

1. S. Ilakkuvanar, *Tholkappiyam in English with Critical Studies* (Madurai: Kuralneri, 1963), Book III, Porul, Seyyuliyal, Verse 489, p. 241.
2. K. Nagarajan, *The Chronicles of Kedaram* (Bombay: Asia, 1961), p. 225.
3. R.K. Narayan, *The Painter of Signs* (Mysore: Indian Thought Publications, 1977), p. 45.
4. R.K. Narayan, *Waiting for the Mahatma* (Mysore: Indian Thought Publications, 1964), p. 118.
5. R.K. Narayan, *The Dark Room* (New Delhi: Orient Paperbacks, 1976), p. 103.
6. R.K. Narayan, *The Vendor of Sweets* (New York: Viking Press, 1967), p. 67.
7. R.K. Narayan, *Swami and Friends* (Mysore: Indian Thought Publications, 1960), p. 59.
8. R.K. Narayan, *The Man-Eater of Malgudi* (Harmondsworth, U.K.: King Penguin, 1983), p. 168.
9. R.K. Narayan, *The Guide* (Mysore: Indian Thought Publications, 1958), p. 12.
10. R.K. Narayan, *The English Teacher* (Mysore: Indian Thought Publications, 1955), p. 109.
11. K.S. Venkataramani, *Murugan, the Tiller* (London: Simpkin, Marshall, Hamilton, Kent, 1927), p. 2.
12. Raja Rao, *Kanthapura* (London: Oxford University Press, 1963), p. 81.
13. Raja Rao, *The Serpent and the Rope* (New York: Pantheon, 1963), p. 274.
14. Raja Rao, *The Cat and Shakespeare* (New York: Macmillan, 1965), p. 67.
15. Kamala Markandaya, *A Silence of Desire* (New York: The John Day Company, 1960), p. 7.
16. Kamala Markandaya, *A Handful of Rice* (New York: The John Day Company, 1960), pp. 211-12.
17 R.K. Narayan, *Mr. Sampath* (Mysore: Indian Thought Publications, 1956), p. 57.
18. Kamala Markandaya, *Nectar in a Sieve* (New York: Signet, 1954), p. 94.
19. Kamala Markandaya, *The Nowhere Man* (New York: The John Day Company, 1972), p. 40.
20. Balachandra Rajan, *The Dark Dancer* (Greenwood Press, 1970), p. 5.
21. Kamala Markandaya, *Possession* (Bombay: Jaico, 1967), p. 26.

The Role of the Guru and Asceticism

8.1. The Significance of the Guru and Asceticism in South India

8.1.1 The Guru as an Embodiment of Knowledge

The role of the Guru in the lives of the people is a fundamental and integral part of the Indian literary and cultural tradition. The South Indian culture shares this with the mainstream of Indian tradition. The Guru occupies the central place in the lives of the people. He is regarded higher than parents. He shows the way to salvation and is able to lead people to the purpose of human existence, of attaining *Mukti.* The Guru is someone in whom knowledge 'Vidya' is personified. 'Vidya' means 'seeing.' The Guru is able to perceive the real and distinguish the real from the unreal. He is personal knowledge available to all the people. He takes the literates as well as the non-literates together. The Guru becomes the key to knowledge and he is the fruit and result of experience, not learning. He is the teacher to whom one can ask questions. The authenticity of the Guru is based on his experience and life. He manifests it in his person. He is the representation of the personal and the spiritual. His significance in society consists in the reaffirmation of the enduring spiritual objectives, exemplified in his person. The need for the Guru is expressed by Raja Rao in *The Serpent and the Rope* through the chief character Ramaswamy: "No, not a God but a Guru is what I need."[1] "The world is either unreal or real—the Serpent or the Rope. . . . One—the Guru—brings you the lantern. The road is seen, the long, white road" (333) Only a Guru can show the path that leads away from one's self. "Ramaswamy's thesis and his love—the two reasons that kept him in France—both being over he turns eastward, back to the origin of his being, to find a deeper meaning of life, an explanation of 'Why we are here, what is it we seek.'"[2] Ramaswamy believes that the answers to these questions can be had from the Guru.

8.1.2 The Guru as an Ascetic

The Guru achieves the enlightened knowledge of life through asceticism. "The ascetic has always played an important role in the social and religious life of Indians. The most venerated characters in the Hindu epics are the ascetics. Heroes like Sri Rama, the Pandavas and the Kauravas never did anything important without consulting these ascetics whom they called Rajgurus. Vashishtha, Drona, Kripacharya were royal counsellors and were held in high esteem. In a country which expects the ideal man to renounce all worldly possessions when he is old and go into the woods for the purification of his soul, it is natural that these ascetics should be treated as the embodiments of wisdom and purity. The Hindu *dharma* envisages four stages in the spiritual growth of a man. Brahmacharya, Grahastha, Vanaprastha and Sanyasa—these four stages are evolutionary, one leading to another. The great religious teachers of India were men who had conquered all the senses and exhorted others to follow suit. Adi Sankara, Ramakrishna Paramhansa, Vivekananda and Sri Aurobindo are the great sons of India who communicated to their countrymen the ecstasy of their spiritual experience. The ascetics are held in high esteem as God's chosen who have done great *sadhana*."[3] R.K. Narayan explains the meaning of the Guru as an ascetic in his introduction to *A Tiger for Malgudi* in which he expresses his fascination for the Guru. An aged tiger escapes from a film shooting camp and wanders into the town. The terror stricken public attempts to get it shot but an ascetic who appears on the scene protects and adopts it as a companion. People ask him the question "Who are you?" he just says "That I am trying to find out." R.K. Narayan uses this scene to describe who a *sanyasi* is: "When one is seized with a passion to habitual modes of thought, one becomes an ascetic; . . . A *sanyasi* is one who renounces everything. . . . Whatever the cause, when one becomes a *sanyasi*, one obliterates one's past. A *sanyasi* is to be taken as he is at the moment. You can never ask a *sanyasi* about his earlier life. He will never refer to it. It would be a crass, inconsiderate act even to ask a *sanyasi* his name. He assumes a new name, bearing no mark of his ancestry or class, but indicative of some general beatitude. He has freed himself from all possessions and human ties. Among certain sects, the man will even perform his own funeral ritualistically before becoming a *sanyasi*. A *sanyasi* is a wanderer living on alms, never rooted to any place except when he seeks the seclusion of a cave or forest at some stage for prolonged meditation."[4] Renunciation and Asceticism become part and parcel of the life and mission of a Guru. The traditional veneration for the ascetic arises mainly out of the popular faith that the ascetic has attained the state of renunciation that other can only aspire for.[5]

8.1.3 The Meaning of Asceticism

Asceticism is a method. It is not an objective. One gives up what is ephemeral and transitory for the higher good. The path of renunciation becomes necessary to know what is real and what is unreal. The attachment to ego, wealth, fame and name get submerged when one begins the quest for the Truth and the divine. Asceticism is a choice. Renunciation is an act of virtue. It is an ideal of life: "be it renunciation of worldly goods and possessions or the renunciation of selfish motive, passion and emotional bondage."[6] It is praised because it signifies the recognition of a greater reality. It is a method by which one can get to that reality.

8.2. The Concern of the Novelists

The importance of the role of the Guru and Asceticism is one of the chief concerns of the Indian English fiction writers. This significant fact is recognized and elaborated by the Indian English fiction critics such as Meenakshi Mukherjee, N. Radhakrishnan, Samares C. Sanyal. They devote separate chapters on this theme in their critical works. Since the above critics follow the thematic approach to Indian English fiction, they consider this theme as a necessary one for the Indian English fiction writer.[7] "The ascetic in the saffron robe is a readymade symbol at the disposal of the Indian novelist and much depends on how he uses this symbol for the purposes of his novel."[8] The selected South Indian novelists are not exceptions to the above fact. They affirm the cultural values of the Guru, his role, the significance of asceticism in South Indian society. They portray the cultural implications of the role of the Guru and asceticism in the following manner in their novels.

a) The respect to the Guru as the symbol of knowledge and renunciation.
b) The influence of the Guru on individuals and people as a whole.
c) The attempts at renunciation by different characters.
d) The transformation that takes place in characters when they become Gurus.

8.2.1 The Respect to the Guru

The Guru is venerated and admired by the people. This is depicted vividly by R.K. Narayan in *The Guide.* The arrival of Raju, the Guru is announced to the people. They come in large numbers to greet him: "Men and women and children arrived in a great mass. All that they wanted was to be allowed to look at him and watch the radiance on his face."[9] The people "loved to bring him gifts. He came to be called Swami by his congregation and where he lived was called the Temple. It was passing into common parlance, 'The Swami said this or that. People loved this place so much that they lime-washed its walls and drew red bands on them.'" (80) The above passage indicates the popularity of Raju, the Guru. Raju refuses and protests to accept the respect of a woman when she attempts to touch his feet, saying: "No human being should ever prostrate before another human being." (93) But the people regard him as an embodiment of knowledge and renunciation: "You are not another human being. You are a Mahatma. We should consider ourselves blessed indeed to be able to touch the dust of your feet." (93) Raju decides to undertake the fast on behalf of the people to implore the almighty for the gift of rain. The people appreciate his great sacrifice: "You are undertaking a great sacrifice Sir, and the least we can do is to be at your side. We derive merit from watching your face." (95) The people believed that "the rains would come down provided the man who performed it was a pure soul, was a great soul. The whole countryside was now in a happy ferment because a great soul had agreed to go through the trial." (95) Velan, the disciple of Raju is all admiration for Raju, the Guru and his wisdom: "Give us a discourse, Sir . . . so that we may have the benefit of your wisdom." (45) Raju declares that he is an ordinary human being and requests Velan not to consider him as a superhuman person: "I am not a saint, Velan. I'm just an ordinary human being like anyone else." (99) This declaration and open confession does not make any impression on Velan: "Velan listened to him without uttering word of surprise or interjection, in all humility. Only he looked a little more serious than usual." (99)

Raman takes Daisy to a hermit who is an old man in *The Painter of Signs* (R.K. Narayan). He is fascinated by the fantastic claims made by this superman and the simple faith of the citizens of the place. He expresses his respect and admiration for this old man: "Just to hear your discourse on life and other matters. You are like an ancient rishi, a rare person to meet, when one meets a great soul and hears his talk, one attains merit, so say the *shastras*."[10]

People come to meet the ascetic who has the tiger as his companion in *A Tiger for Malgudi* (R.K. Narayan). They want to have a *darshan* of this Guru. He objects to this word *darshan*. He invites the people to come inside the cave to meet him without being afraid of the tiger. He declares to them: "I live freely too . . . so there is no place in my system for any rope or chain or bond of any kind." (163) The people do not want to waste the opportunity to visit the Guru. They come forward and place their offerings before the master about which the tiger is proud of:

"Having taken the trouble to come so far, they didn't want to waste the visit and perhaps the feeling that they might encounter the tiger in any case even while retreating, in a short while, they came up and placed their offerings before my master." (163)

Sriram loves Bharati. She is not responding to his love. She is interested in being a faithful disciple of Mahatma Gandhi. She wants to dedicate her life to the independence struggle. Gandhi wants Sriram to hold Bharati as his Guru who deserves respect in *Waiting for the Mahatma* (R.K. Narayan). Mahatma Gandhi exhorts Sriram: "Remember that she is your Guru and think of her with reverence and respect and you will be all right and she will be all right. Sriram took time to digest this sentence."[11]

Ramaswamy's friend Savithri explains her relationship with him in Raja Rao's *The Serpent and the Rope*. She tells her friend Jack: "Ramaswamy has always such interesting things to say about everything. He relates things apparently so unrelated—for him history is a vast canvas, for the discovery of value, of metaphysical value. He's my Guru. . . . A Guru is a real teacher—the one who shows you the way to truth." (180) Savithri treats him with utmost respect.

The examples cited above from the selected South Indian novelists prove an important fact that the Guru is someone who deserves respect and veneration. He is someone special in society, being the embodiment of knowledge, wisdom and experience. He is capable of leading the people to the path of salvation. He is a companion in the journey towards the Truth and God.

8.2.2 The Influence of the Guru

The influence of the Guru on the individuals and the people as a whole is enormous.

The impact of the presence of Raju, the Guru is felt in the community in *The Guide* (R.K. Narayan): "His influence was unlimited. He not only chanted the holy verses and discoursed on philosophy he even came to the stage of prescribing medicine; children who would not sleep peacefully at night were brought to him by their mothers; he pressed their bellies and prescribed a herb, adding, 'If he still gets not relief, bring him again to me.' It was believed that when he stroked the head of a child, the child improved in various ways. Of course, people brought him their disputes and quarrels over the division of ancestral property." (48)

Sarojini, the wife of Dandekar in *A Silence of Desire* (Kamala Markandaya) is almost under the spell of the Swami. Sarojini, a traditional Hindu woman, a good mother and submissive wife, suddenly becomes distant and incomprehensible. She confesses to her husband that the reason for going to the Swami is to be cured of a growth in her womb. When Dandekar asks her why she kept this a secret, Sarojini answers: "Because you would have stopped me going to be healed. . . . Yes, you. You would have sent me to a hospital instead. . . . Call me superstitious, a fool, because I have beliefs that you cannot share."[12] Sarojini has utmost faith in the healing power of the Swami. The presence of the Swami casts a spell not only on Sarojini but also on Dandekar. He himself feels this impact: "When you were with the Swami, actually there, nothing material, or physical mattered. You saw them for the worthless trumperies that they were, rose above your body, knew for a while the meaning of peace." (179) Dandekar feels that the Swami has overpowered Sarojini. He tells his friend Chari: "She's still with me . . . but it's only the shell. All that's real is left with the Swami. Sometimes when I look at her, I know she has even forgotten that I exist. I know in the Swami's world, it is not easy to remember—I've been in it, I know the forgetfulness it brings—but I want to exist, to exist for her. I want my world back, my children happy, my floors swept." (221) Kamala Markandaya portrays the far-reaching influence of the Swami on Sarojini. Meenakshi Mukherjee comments on the role of the Swami in the novel: "The Swami functions not as an individual who lives his own life, but as a public figure—a fulfillment of certain needs of society. He satisfies the needs of the people who want an object of faith." (112)

In the struggle between Lady Caroline and the Swami, to take possession of Valmiki, the shepherd boy-turned-artist, the Swami wins finally, in *Possession* (Kamala Markandaya). Caroline tries her best to allure Valmiki to all sorts of worldly pleasures. His loyalty is with the Swami. The Swami expresses this loyalty emphatically: "He came to me as a child. . . . . He was my disciple during the formative years. Nothing will touch that . . . he will return to me and it will not be the joyless void that you imagine, it will be homecoming."[13] Caroline hands over Valmiki to the Swami in real despair: "Valmiki is yours now but he has been mine." (132) She has the faint hope that Valmiki will come to her again. Meenakshi Mukherjee makes an insightful comment on the character of the Swami: "The Swami of Kamala Markandaya's *Possession* appears vague and shadowy. He is hardly a living character, but he represents the other side in the tug-of-war for the possession of Valmiki. . . . The Swami was Valmiki's guide and mentor before the English woman found him but he makes no claim to him. Eventually however he wins in the tug-of-war because Valmiki after his global tour, fame and publicity, chooses to come back to his obscure South Indian village to the cave where the Swami lives. The conflict here is simple, almost predictable; between possession and renunciation, between wealth and fame on the one hand and freedom and obscurity on the other." (106)

Since people could be easily influenced by the Guru, the gullibility of the people is also exploited. The people of Velan's village are ready to believe Raju as the Guru, without caring to know his past life and exploits: "He decided to look as brilliant as he could manage, let drop gems of thought from his lips, assume all the radiance available and afford them all the guidance they required without stint. He decided to arrange the stage for the display with more thoroughness." (30-31) In K. Nagarajan's *Athawar House,* several chapters are devoted to the description of how a man on the only occasion he came out of the protective orbit of the joint family was duped by an ascetic in Benares. The ascetic systematically went about his job by getting certain photographs of the man taken in a compromising situation and chased him across the country with the intention of blackmailing him.[14] Chandran in the *Bachelor of Arts* (R.K. Narayan) is taken seriously by the people. The people invite him to stay with them. This invitation reflects the gullibility of the people: "Master, our village is so unlucky that few come this way. Bless us with your holy presence for some more days, we beg of you. . . . Master, your very presence will bless our village. we rarely see holy men here. We beg of you to stay for some days more."[15] Thus the influence of the Guru could be positive as well as negative feeding on the gullibility and simple faith of the ordinary people.

8.2.3 The Attempts at Renunciation

The selected novelists also present individuals, who are attempting at the ideal of renunciation. Raja Rao creates credible individuals like Moorthy is *Kanthapura* and Govindan Nair in *The Cat and Shakespeare.* They try to adhere to the ideals of non-attachment, conquest of the senses and selfless love towards all humanity. Moorthy, as a young boy rises above the desires of the flesh and the fear of suffering, of excommunication, and censure of his fellow beings. Moorthy being young still has to fight with himself to achieve equanimity. Moorthy's struggles with himself are often referred to in *Kanthapura.* His attraction to the young widowed girl Ratna is hinted at. He tries to rise above the temptations of the earthly pleasures of life. He overcomes his desire and passion and works with her in the Satyagraha movement in a detached manner. His momentary anguish at being excluded from the social functions of the village and his instinctive revulsion on entering the untouchable Rachanna's house indicate the struggle that went on within him constantly. When he first went to the house of an untouchable and drank milk there, it was in order to test his own capacity to rise above narrow prejudices. Moorthy is young and is still in the process of conquering his senses.[16] His vow of fasting in order to purify himself as well as the society of Kanthapura, indicates the tasks he sets upon himself. His struggle to renounce and rise above the passions and prejudices of average men is appreciated by the villagers: "Moorthy had gone through life like a noble cow, quiet, generous, serene, deferent, brahminic, a very prince. 'He is our Gandhi. Gandhi is the invisible God. Moorthy is the visible Avatar. He is the saint of our village.'"[17]

Govindan Nair in *The Cat and Shakespeare* has crossed the phase of struggle. He has already attained the ideal of renunciation. He has realized the state of *jivan-mukta* which has been defined thus in *Yoga Vashistha*: "The *jivan-mukta* state is that in which the saint has ceased to have any desires. . . . He may be doing all kinds of actions externally, though he remains altogether unaffected by them internally. . . . He is full of bliss and happiness and therefore appears to ordinary eyes to be an ordinary happy man. . . . He is wise and pleasant and loving to all with whom he comes in contact . . . though unaffected within himself, he can take part in the enjoyment of others, he can play like a child and can sympathise with the sorrows of sufferers."[18]

The patriotism and dedication of Kandan in *Kandan, the Patriot* (K.S. Venkataramani) is enhanced by his renunciation. He is venerated as a saint. Pavadi pays a glowing tribute to him: "Kandan is a saint, noble soul, I saw him in his *ashrama* this morning, distributing *charka* and *khaddar* to the suffering poor . . . there's a magnet glow in his eyes, a purifying fire in his speech."[19] Rajee speaks at the funeral of Kandan and points out the nature of his renunciation which has flown into the lives of people as service: "Kandan has died a patriot-saint. Let his *samadhi* rest by the side of the tank in the very coconut garden where the toddy-shop once stood. Let an *ashrama* grow there for rural service, for the uplift and joy of the million poor. Kandan lives the deathless life of a patriot, a martyr." (281)

In Santha Rama Rau's *Remember the House*, the mother is a character who has renounced the possessions of this world, a rich household, an eminent husband and a full life and lives like a recluse far away in a town in Kerala where the Guru lives. The author has employed her not as a living character but as a symbol to counteract the effects of the exuberance and quest of worldly happiness as represented by an American woman.[20]

The renunciation of Chandran in *The Bachelor of Arts* (R.K.

Narayan) is of another kind. R.K. Narayan satirizes this renunciation: "He was different from the usual *sanyasi*. Others may renounce with a spiritual motive or purpose. Renunciation may be to them a means to attain peace or may be peace itself. . . . But Chandran's renunciation was not of that kind. It was an alternative to suicide. . . . He was a *sanyasi* because it pleased him to mortify his flesh. His renunciation was a revenge on society, circumstances and perhaps too on destiny." (176)

The novelists like Raja Rao, R.K. Narayan, K.S. Venkataramani, Santha Rama Rau present renunciation as an ideal worthy to be pursued even by average men and women; it becomes and flows as service of the poor and the downtrodden. It can also become a form of escapism as the result of frustration and disappointment to fly away from the harsh realities of life. Asceticism (renunciation) is a method, not an objective in itself.

8.2.4. The Transformation of Average Men into Gurus

The classical example of the transformation that takes place in an ordinary man when he becomes a Guru is Raju in *The Guide* (R.K. Narayan). This transformation is illustrated by Meenakshi Mukherjee in *The Twice-Born Fiction:* "Raju drifts into the role of a sadhu willy-nilly and once he finds himself cast in the role of an ascetic, he attempts to perform the act with gusto, partly for the sake of self-preservation, partly because it suits his personality wonderfully." (119) Raju never did anything; things always happened to him. He allows himself to be cast in the roles of a tourist guide, an entrepreneur and the business manager of Rosie, the lover of Rosie to win Rosie away from her husband but failed in his attempt; he becomes a convict and performs this role with enthusiasm as an ideal prisoner; he drifts into the role of a sadhu. When he finds that people want to believe in his spiritual power, he cannot disappoint them. He is highly pleased with himself: "No one was more impressed with the grandeur of the whole thing than Raju himself." (42) "He felt that he had worked himself into a position from which he could not get out. He could not betray his surprise." (96)

The selected Indian novelists portray the role of the Guru and asceticism in the following manner; the Guru is presented as an embodiment of knowledge and wisdom based on experience; as an ascetic in whom the ideal of renunciation is exemplified and personified; the Guru is respected and venerated in the South Indian society. He has a unique place and wields enormous influence on the lives of the people. The fake gurus exploit the gullibility and simple faith of the people. The ideal of asceticism is a method used by ordinary men and women to achieve the goal of human existence, *mukti*. Average men and women attempt at renunciation. When an ordinary person becomes a Guru, he goes through transformation and he tries to fit into that role. Thus the novelists confirm the cultural value of the role of the Guru and asceticism in South Indian society, participating in the mainstream of Indian tradition, the eternal awe and fascination for the saffron robe.

NOTES

1. Raja Rao, *The Serpent and the Rope* (New York: Pantheon, 1963), p. 408.
2. Meenakhshi Mukherjee, *The Twice-Born Fiction* (New Delhi: Arnold Heinemann, 1971), p. 97.
3. N. Radhakrishnan, *Indo-Anglian Fiction: Major Trends and Themes* (Madras: Emerald, 1984), pp. 110-11.
4. R.K. Narayan, *A Tiger for Malgudi* (New York: Viking, 1983), pp. 8-9.
5. Meenakhshi Mukerjee, *The Twice-Born Fiction,* p. 99.
6. *Ibid.*, p. 97.
7. Chapter "Renunciation as an Ideal," *Ibid.*, pp. 96-126.
   N. Radhakrishnan, Chapter 6, "The saffron robe," pp. 110-31.
   Samares C. Sanyal *Indianness in Major Indo-English Novels* (Bareilly: Prakash, 1984), Chapter 6: "Anglian Fiction," pp. 205-51.
8. Meenakhshi Mukherjee, *The Twice-Born Fiction*, p. 102.
9. R.K. Narayan, *The Guide* (Mysore: Indian Thought Publications), p. 39.
10. R.K. Narayan, *The Painter of signs* (Mysore: Indian Thought Publications, 1977), p. 75.
11. R.K. Narayan, *Waiting for the Mahatma* (Mysore: Indian Thought Publications, 1964), p. 62.
12. Kamala Markandaya, *A Silence of Desire* (New York: John Day, 1960), p. 107.
13. Kamala Markandaya, *Possession* (Bombay: Jaico, 1967), p. 100.
14. Meenakshi Mukherjee, *The Twice-Born Fiction,* pp. 106-7.
15. R.K. Narayan, *The Bachelor of Arts* (Chicago: The University of Chicago Press, 1980), p. 178.
16. Meenakshi Mukherjee. *The Twice-Born Fiction*, p. 99.
17. Samares C. Sanyal, *Indianness in Major Indo-Anglican Novels,* p. 218.
18. Meenakshi Mukherjee. *The Twice-Born Fiction* pp. 99-100.
19. K.S. Venkataramani, *Kandan, the Patriot* (Madras: Svetaranya Ashrama, 1934), pp. 13-14.
20. Meenakshi Mukherjee, *The Twice-Born Fiction,* p. 99-100.

The Role of Bhakti and the Idea of Religion

9.1. The Role of Bhakti

The direct personal experience of God and the quest for it is known as bhakti in Hindu tradition. The term bhakti is a derivative of the Sanskrit root 'bhaj' to divide, apportion, share. In the religious sphere, bhakti denotes an attitude of devotion on the part of a worshipper to a personal God. In this religious atmosphere devotees are linked with their God and with one another by a bond of 'shared' love and grace. The bhakta's (devotee's) relationship to God is based on the models of a select number of human relations: master-servant; friend-friend; child-parent; the lover and the beloved. In the Tamil context, bhakti is also frequently expressed in the idiom of the relationship between the king and the subject.[1] Bhakti also became a popular religious movement in South India. This could be seen in the innumerable songs sung by Alvars and Nayanmars in praise of their favourite Gods. The aspect of the personal experience of God and the whole-hearted devotion to the divine characterizes the life and culture of the people in South India. The rituals, religious practices and festivals celebrated throughout the year bear witness to this fact. The reverence and devotion with which the pictures and statues of Gods and Goddesses, kept in every household, confirm the role of bhakti in the day to day lives of the people. "Bhakti is certainly a personal and emotional approach to God."[2]

9.2. The Idea of Religion

Religion pervades the entire life and consciousness of the people in South India. To them, religion is a fundamental affirmation of life and it is very personal. Religion becomes an ever present reality. There is the daily reinforcement of the ever present reality of the miracle and also the visual presentation of the exact spot on which the miracle happened in South India. People live in the eternal hope of a miracle. Religion becomes a realistic option. It is verifiable visually and experientially. Hence, religion is not a form of escapism, a mechanism to neutralize pain and to handle life's problems and not a blind superstition. This would be considered as an outsider's perception.

9.3. The Selected Novelists

The novelists chosen for our study have an insider's perception of the role of bhakti and the idea of religion. They articulate the personal experience and devotion to God vividly as an ever present reality which is experienced by the different characters in the novels through the hope of a miracle: pilgrimages; pujas, rituals and practices. They also allude to a few staunch beliefs of the people which may appear to be superstitions for an outsider. These beliefs have an enormous influence and impact on the day-to-day life of the people. We will look at bhakti and religion from these three aspects in this chapter.

a) Bhakti, as a personal experience of God
b) Religion, as an ever present reality
c) The staunch beliefs that have an enormous influence.

9.3.1 Bhakti, as a Personal Experience of God

The novelists portray bhakti as the experience and devotion to particular Gods and Goddesses. R.K. Narayan talks about *Murugan* (Subramaniya) in *The Dark Room.* Ponni comes to meet Savitri in her house after Savitri had been saved by Ponni from suicide. She blesses her with these words: "Murugan's blessings on you. He will protect you and your children."[3] The presence of the temple of Murugan in the town is referred to by R.K. Narayan in the same novel: "The temple had been built fifty years before by a local philanthropist and dedicated to Subramaniya, the peacock-enthroned God, the young son of Shiva." (115) Ramu expresses his faith in the God Murugan by inviting his wife Janaki to go to Palani Hills and worship god Subramaniya in *Murugan, the Tiller* (K.S. Venkataramani): "Janaki, how little religious is your child-mind? Let us go to the Palani Hills and worship there the all-powerful God Subramaniya."[4] Ramakrishna Pai talks about the grandmother of the wife of his friend Mudali who had a great devotion to the Lord Murugan in *The Cat and Shakespeare* (Raja Rao). The grand-daughter of Mudali did not have children and it was the wish of Lord Subramaniya: "Sadhus had blessed and some had even given coconuts with mantras. Nothing happened even after these many holy acts. Well, sit, that is as the Lord Subramaniya wishes."[5] Devotion to Lord Murugan has become part of the religion of the people in Tamilnadu. Fred M.

Clothey comments in the book, *The Many Faces of Murugan:* "Murugan is an expression of Tamil religion. It is a name which evokes many images for Tamil Hindus. Though a celibate, he is the husband of two consorts. He has been hunter, warrior, philosopher. He is teacher and inspiration of literature and arts. He is the eternal child, as old as time itself, yet as young as every new beginning. He is the handsome hero and lover, the wise Primordial One. . . . His exploits have been extolled in both Sanskrit and Tamil literature, including the mythology of epic India and the oldest known Tamil poetry. Known and loved in early Tamil civilization, he has adapted to virtually every significant cultural change in South India, even to the present day. . . . Known also by such names as Skanda, Kumara, Subrahmanya, Kartikeya and Velan. Murugan is one of the most persistent and significant deities of South India."[6] Bhakti becomes personal attachment and surrender to Lord Murugan.

The reference to Lord Nataraja is found in *The Guide, Mr. Sampath* (R.K. Narayan) and *The Dark Dancer* (Balachandra Rajan). Rosie had a personal devotion to Nataraja: "At one corner of the room, she'd have a bronze figure of Nataraja, the god of dancers, the God whose primal dance created the vibrations that set the worlds in motion."[7] The grandmother of Srinivas had given him a statue of Nataraja when he was a boy in *Mr. Sampath:* "The carving represented Nataraja with one foot raised and one foot pressing down a demon, his four arms outstretched, with his hair flying, the eyes rapt in contemplation, an exquisitely poised figures. His grandmother had given to him on his eighth birthday. . . . It had never left Srinivas since that birthday. . . . It had become part of him, this little image. He often sat before it, contemplated its proportions and addressed it everyday. It had been his first duty for decades now. He never started his day without spending a few minutes before this image."[8] Krishnan explains to Cynthia, his lover, the significance of Nataraja in *The Dark Dancer:* "There is the great Nataraja at Chidambaram, infinite energy and infinite repose."[9] Krishnan himself has experienced the power of this God when he heard His praises sung during the festivities: "He saw the great figure of the Nataraja, one leg arched in the supreme expression of energy, the dying smile of the demon, beneath the other's lightness, all that infinite power of destruction drawn back into the bronze circle of repose." (28)

Sushila, the wife of Krishnan, in *The English Teacher* has a tremendous faith in the protection and benevolence of Lord Srinivasa. Krishnan admires her devotion: "There on a pedestal she kept a few silver images of gods and covered them with flowers; two small lamps were lit before them every morning. I often saw her standing there with the light in her face, her eyes closed and her lips tightly moving."[10] Sushila loves to visit the temple of Srinivasa in town: "Srinivasa the greatest God; you need not visit Tirupathi Hills to see him, if you visit him here—he grants all your boons and blesses all your efforts." (69)

Lord Ganesha is respected in Tamil households. People have a special devotion. This personal devotion is referred to in *Murugan, the Tiller* (K.S. Venkataramani), *The Dark Dancer* (Balachandra Rajan). When Thoppal, Murugan, a robber chieftain, escape from jail, they go to the temple of Ganesha to pay their respects in *Murugan, the Tiller*: "there was a little temple of Ganesha in which an oil-lamp still fed of a dying flame. The three went silently and prostrated before the elephant God." (20) The mother of Krishnan has a personal attachment to Lord Ganesha *(The Dark Dancer)*. She wants to take her son to temple after he comes back from abroad safely: "All of us wanted to take you to the temple, all together and thank Lord Ganesha for your safe return—Now it cannot be done. You have been away a long time and don't know what it means to us." (7) The mother of Krishnan expresses her fear and apprehension that he would have lost touch with this devotion since he had been so many years abroad.

K. Nagarajan describes through Koni, the narrator of the novel, the tremendous devotion and enthusiasm of the people in Kedaram to the deity Kedareswar in *Chronicles of Kedaram:* "It is amazing how much Kedareswar has become a part of our lives. Not a small part, mind you, but quite a big part, almost the whole of it. . . . Kedareswar is not a feared deity but a beneficent, kindly god, near at hand, ready to respond to the call of the devotees and one who has held . . . physical converse with many of those whose faith was firm, deep-rooted and sincere."[11] This passage brings out the intimate relationship of the deity with the people.

Raja Rao articulates the hold and the influence of Goddess Kenchamma on the people of Kanthapura in *Kanthapura.* The people almost possess her as their own. They have the Sthala Purana about her: "Kenchamma is our goddess. Great and bounteous is she. She killed a demon ages ago, a demon that had come to ask our young sons as food and our young women as wives. Kenchamma came from the Heavens—it was the sage Tripura who had made penances to bring her down—and she waged such a battle and she fought so many a night that the blood soaked and soaked into the earth and that is why, the Kenchamma Hill is all red."[12]

The devotion to gods and goddesses is practised by keeping their statues and hanging their pictures on the wall and painting them in the temples. The artist Chinna Dorai talks to Jagan of this custom in *The Vendor of Sweets* (R.K. Narayan): "The figures of Shiva, the destroyer,

Vishnu, the protector, Devi, who vanquished the demon Mahisha with the dreadful weapons she bore in her eighteen arms and the Dwarapalakas, gatekeepers at the shrine and the designs on the doorways and friezes on the walls were all alike done by my master, all over the South."[13]

The role of bhakti in the lives of the people, its pervasineness, and effectiveness are brought out by Balachandra Rajan in *The Dark Dancer*. Krishnan tells the story of Nanda, to Cynthia, to illustrate the fact that bhakti has the power even to move the Gods: "Nanda was a pariah. The priests wouldn't allow him even on the steps of the temple. But he prayed and prayed and because of the strength of his devotion to God, the statue of Nandi, the great bull, moved aside, so that he could see the dancing image of Shiva." (131)

The selected novelists portray bhakti and its vital role in the lives of the people as a personal and emotional approach to God as we have seen above in the portrayal of personal attachment to Gods and Goddesses like Murugan, Lord Nataraja, Lord Srinivasa, Lord Ganesha, Kedareswar, Kenchamma. Bhakti has its own logic in the minds and hearts of the people in South India. It has a great power as is demonstrated in the story of Nanda.

9.3.2 Religion as an Ever Present Reality

People in South India live with the sense and expectation of a miracle. Their familiarity with the Gods and Goddesses could be seen in the vows and votive offerings they offer to them. They almost bargain with the deities.

This sense of the miracle is found in an ordinary rustic woman like Rukmani in *Nectar in a Sieve* (Kamala Markandaya). She expresses her deep faith in the divine when her son Kuti is slowly getting well. They had given up all hope for his survival. She believes that because of her earnest prayers, he is recovering: "Gods were not remote, not unheedful since they had heard his cries and stilled them as it were by a miracle."[14]

Rukmani wanted desperately a male child. Her husband Nathan also was worried. They had the fear that Ira would be their only child. She prayed earnestly to the Gods, hoping for a miracle: "My mother whenever I paid her a visit, would make me accompany her to the temple and together we would pray and pray before the deity, imploring for help until we were giddy." (22)

Ambika does not bear a child for a long time. Ambika and her husband Jagan are taken to the temple on Badri Hill with the expectation of a miracle in *The Vendor of Sweets* (R.K. Narayan). The novelist puts this sense of religion as an ever present reality in the minds and hearts of people in this short sentence: "The temple is known as Sanatana Krishna; a visit to it is the only known remedy for barrenness in women." (163)

People of Kanthapura live in constant hope of the help and protection of the Goddess Kenchamma. They woo her for favours with vows and votive offerings. Rangamma prays in *Kanthapura* earnestly for the release of Moorthy: "Rangamma vowed she would offer a kanchi sari to Kenchamma if he were released and Ratna said she would have a thousand and eight flames ceremony performed and Nanjamma said she would give the goddess, a silver belt and Pariah Rachanna said he would walk the holy fire and all said, 'the Goddess will never fail us—she will free him from the clutches of the Red-man.'" (133) Religion becomes an affirmation of life. It becomes a living reality expressed in the personal faith and the firm hope that the goddess will not let them down. The familiarity with the deity is revealed in the bargaining relationship for favours bestowed.

The little boy Swami in *Swami and Friends* (R.K. Narayan) is not an exception to the above fact. He bargains in his own way. He loses the way in darkness and is unable to come back home: "He prayed to all the Gods that he knew, to take him out of that place. He promised them offerings: two coconuts every Saturday to the elephant-faced Ganapathi; a vow to roll bare-bodied in dust, beg, take the alms to the Lord of Tirupathi. He paused as if to give the Gods time to consider his offer and descend from their heights to rescue him."[15]

The sense of ever present reality of religion is expressed in the ardent desire of people in undertaking pilgrimages to Benares and other holy places. The grandmother of Sriram wants to go to Benares to end her days in peace. She considers it a great grace in *Waiting for the Mahatma* (R.K. Narayan): "She is with a number of others, who spend their last years there, old persons who are waiting to die. They cheerfully await their death and look forward to the final fire and the final ablution in the sacred Ganges."[16] The Aunt of Raman is lost in the vision of her pilgrimage to Badrinath. She is almost in ecstasy in *The Painter of Signs* (R.K. Narayan): "A *darshanam* of the god in Badrinath and if possible to Amarnath, where the *lingam* is shaped in ice. I wouldn't care what happened to me or to the world after I have seen the holy places and dipped into the Ganges from its birthplace all along its course, until I end my pilgrimage in Benares. After this I shall want nothing more in life." The pilgrimage to Benares is the crown and fulfillment of one's life of faith. It is a dream of so many orthodox Hindus even to-day in

South India.

The pilgrimage to Tirupathi is undertaken with all devotion and preparation by Margayya in *The Financial Expert* to obtain the favour of good health for his son Balu. The elder brother of Margayya explains to him the rigorous preparation to go for the pilgrimage: "The God at Tirupathi does not like anyone to visit him as a holiday-maker, just for fun. He wants you to go there as a humble suppliant, in the attitude of a beggar . . . that's the symbol, that's why you are obliged to visit at least ten houses with a begging bowl, stand and cry at the door for alms and then go on to the pilgrimage, on foot, if possible. The god does not notice a person who goes to him in a holiday mood."[17] Margayya expresses his utmost satisfaction in completing the pilgrimage successfully: "He remembered how he carried the alms and the sovereigns equal to the weight of the child to the Tirupathi Hills and deposited them all in the treasure box in the shrine. He felt he had done a good job, and it had been an enchanting pilgrimage." (132)

The ever-present reality of religion and its consciousness is revealed in the lives of the people through their eternal hope of miracle and the untiring devotion with which they undertake pilgrimages from the above examples cited from the selected novelists.

9.3.3 The Staunch Beliefs that have an Enormous Influence

People believe in certain practices and have staunch belief in them. To an outsider, they look irrational and superstitious. It is very difficult to draw the dividing line between blind belief and faith. This is articulated through his character Gupta in *The Painter of Signs* (R.K. Narayan) when Gupta warns Daisy about the beliefs of the people: "Superstition, faith, the working of real incalculable forces, all three operate in our country, but we can never be certain where one begins and the other ends . . . we are in a mixed-up state. Social workers have to take this into account." (113)

Margayya wants to become a rich man. He is ready to swallow anything that the priest tells him. They become staunch beliefs of Margayya in *The Financial Expert* (R.K. Narayan). The priest speaks about the importance of the planet Saturn: "Do you know that Saturn is the most powerful entity in the world? and if he is gratified, he can make you a ruler of this world or he can just drown you in an ocean of misery. Nobody can escape him. Better keep him in good humour." (45)

The priest convinces him of the need for rituals to obtain favours from Gods and goddesses: "the Shastras lay down such and such rituals for such and such ends. Between a man who performs them and one who doesn't the chances are greater for the former. That's all I can say." (46) The priest asks Margayya to repeat the prayer to Goddess Lakshmi who presides over wealth, distinction, bravery and enterprise and all the good things in life. He should repeat the prayer at least a thousand times. Margayya takes him seriously: "Every day it took him eight hours of repetition to complete the thousand and then he reverently put the black paste on his forehead, lit the camphor, called in his wife and child and sprinkled the holy water on them. His jaws ached, his tongue had become dry . . . he felt faint with hunger, since he had to fast completely while praying." (57) The practices mentioned above highlight the magical element of religion. Many people follow numerous practices like the ones above in South India.

The practice of exorcism is found in the novels. R.K. Narayan gives an elaborate description of this practice and the staunch belief of the people in *The English Teacher* and *Mr. Sampath.* The mother-in-law of Krishnan *(The English Teacher)* is convinced that the Evil Eye had fallen on her daughter, Sushila, and at the new house a malignant spirit had attacked her. She arranged with the help of the cock for an exorcist to visit the house. He is respected as a Swamiji: "He felt her pulse. He uttered some mantras with closed eyes, took a pinch of sacred ash and rubbed it on her forehead and tied to her arm a talisman strong in yellow thread." (93) Even the doctor who comes to visit Sushila acknowledges the belief of the common people in wandering mystics like the swamiji: "There is a lot in him too, we don't know. When we understand it fully. I am sure we doctors will be able to give more complete cures." (93)

The mother of Ravi in *Mr. Sampath* takes him to an exorcist to get rid of his mental disease. She firmly believes in the power of the exorcist. She tells the friend of Ravi, Srinivas: "Shall I take Ravi to the temple at Sailam? It is a day's journey from here. The exorcist says that if Ravi is kept there at its portals for a week, he will be quite well. There are hundreds of people living there." (208)

The reference to Evil Eye and its impact are described by Kamala Markandaya in A *Silence of Desire.* Rajam attributes evil eye to the sickness of Dandekar. She gives an allusion to the disease of Aunt Sita: "it was the evil eye of the neighbour who coveted the diamond nose screw that she wore."[18] A lot of people in South India consider the reason for suffering and sickness as the evil eye of the neighbours.

Raman wants to know whether Daisy will be his in *The Painter of Signs* (R.K. Narayan) and he expects a sign from the Goddess. The old man in the temple explains to him the accidental action of the dropping of a single flower. He tells Raman: "Did you notice the single flower that fell down from the crown? That's an omen—which means success, but trouble before and after." (77)

This is not an exhaustive list of the staunch beliefs and religious practices of the people in South India. The impact of the evil eye, exorcism, and the magical element of religion are chosen to demonstrate the influence they have on people. To the outsiders, these may look as superstitions but the people who practice them, consider those practices as real and they believe in them.

The role of bhakti and the idea of religion are vast subjects of the culture and life of the people in South India. The aspects that have been shown as cultural values of the role of bhakti and the idea of religion are the personal devotion and surrender to individual gods and goddesses; religion as an ever-present reality with the hope and expectation of a miracle, supplemented by pilgrimages and votive offerings: the practices of exorcism, recitation of mantra and the impact of the evil eye. The selected novelists allude to the three aspects above in some of their novels.

NOTES

1. Norman Cutler, *Songs of Experience: The Poetics of Tamil Devotion* (Bloomington: Indiana University Press, 1987), Introduction, p. 1
2. Kamil Zvelebil, *The Smile of Murugan* (Leiden, Netherlands: E.J. Brill, 1973), p. 195.
3. R.K. Narayan, *The Dark Room* (New Delhi: Orient Paperbacks, 1976), p. 125.
4. K.S. Venkataramani, *Murugan, the Tiller* (London: Simpkin, Marshall, Hamilton Kent, 1927), p. 195.
5. Raja Rao, *The Cat and Shakespeare* (New York: Macmillan, 1965), p. 58.
6. Fred M. Clothey, *The Many Faces of Murugan* (The Hague, Netherlands: Mouton, 1978), p. 1.
7. R.K. Narayan, *The Guide* (Mysore: Indian Thought Publications 1958), p. 108.
8. R.K. Narayan, *Mr. Sampath* (Mysore: Indian Thought Publications, 1956), p. 19.
9. Balachandra Rajan, *The Dark Dancer* (Westport, U.S.A.: Greenwood Press, 1970), p. 84.
10. R.K. Narayan, *The English Teacher* (Mysore: Indian Thought Publications, 1955), p. 37.
11. K. Nagarajan, *Chronicles of Kedaram* (Bombay: Asia, 1961), p. 41.
12. Raja Rao, *Kanthapura* (London: Oxford University Press, 1963), p. 2.

13. R.K. Narayan, *The Vendor of Sweets* (New York: Viking, 1967), p. 100.
14. Kamala Markandaya, *Nectar in a Sieve* (New York: Signet, 1954), p. 98.
15. R.K. Narayan, *Swami and Friends* (Mysore: Indian Thought publications, 1960), p. 160.
16. R.K. Narayan, *Waiting for the Mahatma* (Mysore: Indian Thought Publications, 1964), p. 138.
17. R.K. Narayan, *The Financial Expert,* (New York: Noonday Press, 1964), pp. 131-32.
18. Kamala Markandaya, *A Silence of Desire* (New York: John Day, 1969), p. 210.

Part V

Kanthapura to Malgudi

Discussion on Indian English literature and its problems gave us a meaningful backdrop for the whole book. The exposition of the critical approaches taken to analyse and evaluate the Indian English fiction provided the literary context for the sharpening and focusing of the cultural approach. The definition and clarification of the terms: Culture, Values, Assumptions, selected South Indian Novelists, pointed to the specificity and particularity of the book i.e. discovering, interpreting and evaluating the South Indian cultural element (the strong regional element) in the selected South Indian novelists in English. The rest of the parts demonstrated the experimental verification of the above paradigm through a detailed analysis of the chosen cultural values and assumptions such as

1. The idea and role of womanhood
2. The significance of relationship
3. The role of myths and puranas
4. The absorption of native expressions, proverbs, customs and festivals into the narrative
5. The role of the Guru and asceticism
6. The role of bhakti and the idea of religion.

Based on this analysis, I would like to suggest the following critical observations and enumerate the advantages of this specific and particular approach taken in the book to make the cultural study of the novels, more pointed and focused.

1. A novel in English, written by a South Indian author has its lasting value and intrinsic worth in so far as it reflects and represents authentically and truly, the culture of the people. Hence the content of the novel takes precedence over the form of the novel which may be a finished or an experimental one. Thus the novel becomes a document and treasury of cultural knowledge.
2. The extension and focusing of the regional element in the cultural approach to Indian English fiction helps us to avoid sweeping and vague generalizations about "Indianness" and gives us a clear grasp and

understanding of this concept in a concrete and tangible way. The book illustrates a significant fact that a meaningful and useful discussion on "Indianness" is not possible without paying attention to the strong regional element present in the novels.

3. It is highly profitable to apply the above study to identify the strong regional cultural values so that the pan-Indian cultural values obtain a specific reference and locus to a particular area instead of remaining vague, general and nebulous.
4. The perception of the values and assumptions of South Indian culture is characterized by closeness and earthiness by writers like R.K. Narayan, K.S. Venkataramani and K. Nagarajan who have spent most of their lives in South India and have become part and parcel of this culture. They write with certain amount of authority. The novels become primarily vehicles of self-expression, though written in a foreign language.
5. This perception could be contrasted with the perception of writers like Raja Rao, Kamala Markandaya, Santha Rama Rau and Balachandra Rajan. The perception of the above writers is characterized by nostalgia and longing for the values of their native land since they have spent most of their lives abroad. The novels become primary vehicles of communication with the Western audience.
6. In the hands of R.K. Narayan, K.S. Venkataramani and K. Nagarajan, the English language itself gets indigenized, integrated and fused into the text of the novels by the absorption of proverbs, expressions, customs and festivals from the native languages and culture. Raja Rao also attempts this to a certain extent. The absorption in R.K. Narayan, K.S. Venkataramani and K. Nagarajan is spontaneous, natural and without much effort.
7. The use of myths and puranas gives us a glimpse of the consciousness of the writers who are steeped in Indian tradition and the strong regional cultural element comes to the fore by the sthala puranas.
8. The perception of the selected South Indian novelists in English of South Indian cultural values and assumptions is essentially urbanized, anglicized and elitistic. They touch on middle class problems. They do not sufficiently take into account the 'little tradition' and the problems that affect the poor and the low castes. Certainly, their portrayal of poverty, exploitation, untouchability and caste discrimination may be sympathetic and concerned but it lacks the authentic voice of the poor and the oppressed.

Obviously, this book is not an exhaustive study. The book has stopped with identifying a few South Indian cultural values and assumptions. It has attempted a limited analysis of them. The nature and quality of these values and the native sources from which these values emerge, could be studied and explored. This study indicates a step forward in the criticism of Indian English fiction of evolving our own criterion to judge and evaluate the novels in English written in South India rather than unduly depending on the principles of criticism imported from the West. A paradigm has been evolved. An experimental verification and a limited application of the paradigm has been illustrated in the study of the seven authors and their thirty-six novels. The same paradigm could be used in the study of Indian English fiction short-story, prose, drama and poetry in the future.

Index